GILLY
the
GHILLIE

Praise for *Gilly the Ghillie*

"A delightful and entertaining tale that captures our (often eccentric) West Coast island communities, complete with gum boots, pot plants, fish gutting, wood stoves, and salty, blustery storms. Makes me want to get a fishing guide and go fishing!"

ANNY SCOONES bestselling author of *Island Home: Out and About on Vancouver Island*

"A winningly entertaining set of linked stories concerning the lives of fishing guides and their clients along the upper BC coast. The foibles of characters such as Baba, Troutbreath, and the eponymous Gilly, along with the author's understated dry humour, beg the question—what will they get up to next?"

DON HUNTER author of the Stephen Leacock Medal–shortlisted *Spinner's Inlet* and *Return to Spinner's Inlet*

"You invite a handful of Very Important Writers to a large formal dinner to hear their stories. For some reason, a fishing guide is at the table, too. By dinner's end, everyone is rolling around laughing at the guide's stories. Ladies and gents, meet David Giblin, storyteller of Stuart Island…"

JAMIE LAMB author of *Christmas in Mariposa*

"The lives of fishing guides on Stuart Island are every bit as complex, quirky, and turbulent as the tidal rapids and whirlpools they negotiate daily in search of enormous salmon. David Giblin's engaging, often funny, tales effectively portray life on BC's wild waters and remote islands."

JOY DAVIS author of *Complicated Simplicity: Island Life in the Pacific Northwest*

Praise for *The Codfish Dream*

"You'll meet eccentric shore workers, wealthy guests who arrive by yacht and floatplane, as well as essential guides Big Jake, Lucky Petersen, Vop and Wet Lenny... A deadpan narrative keeps the absurdity coming as earnest RCMP, FBI, and Fisheries officers encounter the salmon-obsessed denizens of the island resort. This book is a keeper."

DAVID CONN *Western Mariner*

"*The Codfish Dream* is a lively read with many layers. Those who fish will no doubt identify with the chronicles of the fish and those who pursue them."

KENNETH CAMPBELL *Ormsby Review*

"David Giblin is a marvellous storyteller, and *The Codfish Dream* is a wonderful book: witty, whimsical, well-written, and a terrific read from cover to cover."

IAN FERGUSON author of *The Survival Guide to British Columbia* and winner of the Stephen Leacock Medal for *Village of the Small Houses*

"As skillful a writer as he was a sports-fishing guide, David Giblin deftly hooks, reels, and lands us in the watery world of Canada's wild west coast of the 1980s. Each cleverly crafted story offers a porthole view into a rollicking season of unforgettable characters, capturing a time and place changed forever. With insights and humour as finely honed as a dressing knife, we walk a mile in his gumboots in the hunt for the mighty tyee salmon."

SYLVIA TAYLOR author of *Beckoned by the Sea* and *The Fisher Queen*

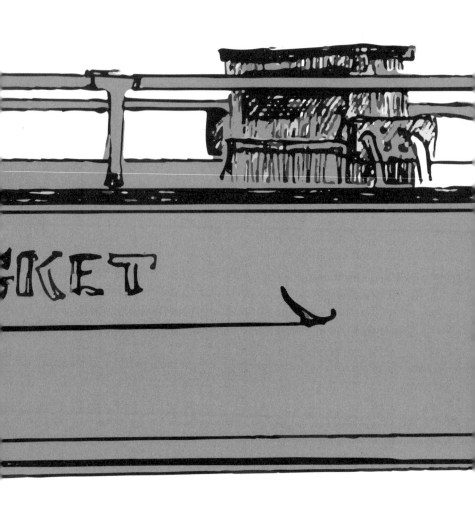

David Giblin

GILLY
the
GHILLIE

More CHRONICLES OF A
WEST COAST FISHING GUIDE

Heritage House Publishing Company Ltd.
heritagehouse.ca

Cataloguing information available from Library and Archives Canada

978-1-77203-335-9 (pbk)
978-1-77203-336-6 (ebook)

Edited by Lenore Hietkamp
Proofread by Nandini Thaker
Cover and interior design by Jacqui Thomas
Cover image by David Giblin

Dictionary definition on p. xi is adapted from *Dictionary*, Mac G4 ed., v. 2.0.3 (51.5). Apple Inc., 2005–2007.

Excerpt from Vancouver's log on p. 175 is from *The Voyage of George Vancouver, 1791–1795: Volumes I–IV*, edited by W. Kaye Lamb (London: Hakluyt Society, 1984)

The interior of this book was produced on 100% post-consumer recycled paper, processed chlorine free, and printed with vegetable-based inks.

Heritage House gratefully acknowledges that the land on which we live and work is within the traditional territories of the Lkwungen (Esquimalt and Songhees), Malahat, Pacheedaht, Scia'new, T'Sou-ke, and W̱SÁNEĆ (Pauquachin, Tsartlip, Tsawout, Tseycum) Peoples.

We acknowledge the financial support of the Government of Canada through the Canada Book Fund (CBF) and the Canada Council for the Arts, and the Province of British Columbia through the British Columbia Arts Council and the Book Publishing Tax Credit.

24 23 22 21 20   1 2 3 4 5

Printed in Canada

For Blake

CONTENTS

Ghillie
noun
variant spelling of *gillie*.
|'gilē| |'gɪli|

1. (in Scotland) a man or boy who attends someone on a hunting or fishing expedition.
· *historical*: a Highland chief's attendant.

2. (usu. *ghillie*) a type of shoe with laces along the instep and no tongue, esp. those used for Scottish country dancing.

ORIGIN Late 16th century, from Scottish Gaelic *gille*, "lad, servant." The word was also found in the term *gilliewetfoot*, denoting a servant who carried the chief over a stream, used as a contemptuous name by Lowlanders for the follower of a Highland chief.

Sense 2 dates from the 1930s.

 *one* **THE LOOSE CANNON**

ALL NIGHT THE storm had been building. Nelson was roused from a deep sleep several times by strange sounds. When a grey dawn finally broke, ragged black clouds scudded past and small branches were already being stripped from the trees. A cruel wind swept the rain and sleet before it. The sound of the rain pelting the picture window filled the living room.

It was that kind of morning. Why get out of a warm and dry bed when the wind was blowing a gale? The guests weren't due to arrive for another couple of weeks, and all the preparations were well in hand. Just roll over and go back to sleep. Of course, Nelson found that impossible to do.

He lay in bed and listened to the sounds of the storm, sorting through them to try to figure out what had woken him. Most were familiar—rain on the windows and skylights, the cracking of branches giving way in the wind; all pretty standard. From farther away came the usual creaking of the docks below as they rose and fell and rubbed against the pilings.

The docks were empty, and no large yachts were straining at their lines, in danger of breaking loose. A great deal of work had been done over the the winter to build up the existing docks. A new finger float had been added for a couple of returning big yachts—almost overbuilt, Nelson mused. The metal walkway that led down to the docks squeaked, and he made a mental note to add more grease to its roller. None of these noises would have been enough to wake him.

Still, there must be something going on. He finally forced himself out of the warm bed to have a look. He walked sleepily out of the manager's bedroom at the back of the main lodge into the guest lounge and stopped in front of the large picture window overlooking the front deck, the docks below, and the rest of the resort property.

Nelson yawned and stretched, adjusting his flannel pajamas. Things looked pretty secure and tidy. He felt pleased with himself.

He had almost forgotten about the new satellite TV. A satellite dish—the largest one Herbert could find, over ten feet in diameter—sat on the deck. Herbert and a couple of people had arrived on Herbert's yacht two days ago with the whole system. They hauled up the TV that now had pride of place in the lounge. All the supporting technology was arranged on the shelves under the picture window. There had been much fiddling to point the dish to the correct azimuth, a word Herbert liked to hear himself saying. Getting the angles right had consumed most of their time.

If Herbert hadn't carried on about it, Nelson might have turned away from the window and headed back to bed. But he peered through the rain, then folded his arms and frowned. The angle of the dish wasn't right.

As the wind gusted again, something terrible happened. Like a hooded raptor, the dish turned slightly, facing Nelson. Then the wind blew full on and sent it skidding across the deck toward him. Toward him and the precious plate-glass window, which was the only thing that stood between Nelson and the giant satellite dish. Nelson jumped back instinctively.

As the dish hurtled toward him, it made the sound that had disturbed his sleep.

He had an ice-cold realization. The metal monster had spent the early-morning hours roaming around because Herbert and the others had neglected to secure it to the deck. Nelson had watched them drill the holes for the lag bolts, heavy, five-inch-long metal pegs that would keep the dish in place. It was the last thing to do after they had gotten the dish where they wanted it. Obviously, they never finished the job.

That precious window also protected the massive new television—a full thirty-two-inch screen—and all the electronics to make it run, as well as the latest audio gear for playing music. If the dish smashed the window, the rain currently pelting the world outside would ruin the entire expensive system.

To the left of the window, in the hallway leading to the hot tub just outside the door, hung a bright yellow bathrobe above a pair of gumboots. Nelson pulled on the boots and grabbed the robe, with its red monogram, "iv." Vop had been over to use the hot tub the night before, and he'd left his robe behind. Nelson stepped out the door.

The gusting wind had brought the dish close to the edge of the deck. He used the thin cotton belt of the bathrobe to tie it to the railing, hoping it would hold while he went to the generator shed for the tools and equipment to fix this mess.

Nelson hunched into the wind, clutching the bright yellow, monogrammed bathrobe closed with both hands. The wind found all the places to push aside his loose flannel pajamas and drive the cold rain into his skin. He made slow headway uphill, toward the tool shed and against the windstorm. The gumboots he had grabbed in his hurry were a couple sizes too big, and his feet slipped around inside them.

He muttered as he struggled, and the wind picked up and scattered his words. "'Installation experts,' my ass. Just a couple of his useless drinking buddies he didn't want his wife to know about. That poor woman, not a goddamned jury in the land would convict either of us, no matter how bloody we left his corpse."

He pulled the collar of Vop's bathrobe even tighter to his chin. The gumboots slapped painfully against his soaked, pajama-clad legs. He had to fight for every step up the plank walkway. The wind grew stronger as he pushed through the gusts, and he was now being pelted with debris ripped from the trees, along with the driving rain. He knew what the increasing strength of the wind was doing on the deck, and settled into his struggle with a grim determination.

Finally arriving at the tool shed, Nelson threw open the door and started sorting through several buckets he had used to organize his last job. He found the one he wanted and upended it. Heavy lag bolts left over from building the new docks clattered onto the floor. Nelson scooped up four or five before they stopped rolling and tossed them back into the bucket. He threw in a heavy hammer and a socket wrench that fit the bolts, and then pulled a coil of rope over his shoulder. He paused for a moment to make sure he had everything he needed.

Satisfied, he turned and left the shed, one hand lugging the bucket and the other clutching the collar of the bathrobe. He hugged the bucket to his chest for whatever comfort it could provide. At least the wind was at his back, for now. As he staggered back to the resort, Nelson sounded like a small herd of Swiss milk cows as the contents of his bucket clanged around inside it.

The walkway led into the shelter of the rocky bank just above the front deck of the resort, where the satellite dish waited. The wind backed off a little, a dramatic pause that allowed Nelson to stop for a moment and catch his breath.

So far, the narrow cotton belt was holding, although the material was obviously stretched to the breaking point. Nelson knew it needed just one more burst of wind for it to give in completely. As he left the shelter of the rocks and stepped out onto the deck, the full force of rain and wind threw its arms around him like an old friend. The dish sensed him approaching and heaved and bucked against the thin yellow restraint. Nelson was almost there, rope in hand, when that tortured bit of cotton finally let go. Suddenly free, the dish leapt toward him. Nelson was between it and the plate-glass window, and stepping out of the way was not an option. With the rope over his shoulder and the bucket still in his hands, he jumped onto the thing.

The dish skittered toward the window. Nelson heard someone screaming, but the wind ripped the sound away. He held on, but had to drop the bucket. Its contents rolled onto the deck. His weight hardly slowed the dish. Together, they charged across the deck right at the plate glass. Not so much a rider as a reluctant passenger, Nelson was carried along helplessly on the back of this metal beast.

He remembered something he had read recently in an issue of the *National Geographic*. Herbert left them scattered around the lounge; he thought they gave the place a touch of the outdoor intellectual. A paleoanthropologist in one article wrote about trying to understand the pattern of bone injuries suffered by the Neanderthals. Scientists thought it might be related to their hunting practices but wanted to confirm it somehow. They first looked at modern-day occupations that they thought might be similar to the activities of those hunters, like rodeo riders. It wasn't until they looked at the lowly rodeo clown who protected the riders that they found a pattern of injuries that bore a striking resemblance to those of the Neanderthal hunters. The hunters and the clowns both were trying to survive, and maybe help out their fellow man at the same time. They had to stand on the ground while large, angry animals charged at them. They were kicked, stomped, run over, gored, and thrown into the air, and sometimes the only thing to do was to grab hold of the thing charging them and hold on. All of which left a tale of broken bones.

With a winter's worth of beard and wearing his ridiculous yellow and red outfit, Nelson thought he must have looked a bit of both clown and Neanderthal. He smiled grimly as he closed his eyes and waited for the pain to start.

Nothing happened. Nelson felt a gentle deceleration and then everything just came to a stop. Carefully, slowly, as if even the mere movement of his eyelids would fling him into a jagged glass chasm, Nelson opened his eyes. His insane Neanderthal clown reflection stared at him from the plate glass, mere inches away. The wind had died.

Reprieved for the moment, Nelson knew it could return, even stronger. He slid down and began wrestling with the inanimate dish again. It had taken Herby and two other men to put the dish in place yesterday. Nelson felt very alone out on the front deck of the resort today.

The dish, which only moments ago had skittered across the deck trying to attack him, now resisted doing anything at all. It had returned to its immovable metal state. He couldn't push or pull it. However, he found he could rock the dish by using as leverage the arms and crosspieces he had been clinging to moments before. He worked it slowly back, an inch at a time, to its original position. He could see the waiting holes in the deck, but then something else caught his eye.

Out on the water was a lone guide boat, moving through the storm on a straight course for the resort. Sometimes it disappeared, hidden by the blowing spray. Its slow but relentless progress distracted Nelson. He couldn't believe anyone could be out on the water on such a wretched morning. Some urgent mission must be driving them into the bite of wind and spray.

The dish saw its opportunity. It seemed to raise its head and turn. Nelson caught the movement out of the corner of his eye and stepped to one side. The dish followed. Nelson stopped to see what it would do next. The dish stopped. Nelson took a step toward it. He still hoped he could tie it off on the rail, and the dish had just moved closer to it. Then the wind gusted from a different direction. The dish stepped into the centre of the deck. It was mocking Nelson. It turned slightly in the wind with almost a come-hither look.

Nelson moved toward it. The dish moved away again, back toward the railing. Another gust of wind, stronger than any so far that morning, caught the dish and it flew along the railing toward the window once more. It was trying to do an end run around Nelson. Nelson threw himself onto its back again. The wind hurled them toward the window. From somewhere, Nelson heard someone screaming again. He would have to look into that, but right now he was far too busy.

In the days of sail-powered warships with muzzle-loaded cannons, sometimes, in a heavy sea, a ship's gun might break loose. It could maim and kill sailors and even punch holes in the hull of a ship and sink it. To slow a gun's movement across the gun deck, the crew would throw down ropes, hammocks, timbers, and blocks—anything to save the ship from such a terror. Mostly, such attempts at impediments were simply mashed into a pulp, but today, Nelson got lucky. As the dish was being pushed along the railing, it ran up on one of the lag bolts from the bucket Nelson had dropped onto the deck, which had gotten stuck in a gap between the deck boards. The thrust of the dish forced the bolt deeper into the wood.

His tormentor's sudden stop threw Nelson onto the deck. He sprang back up as fast as the gumboots would let him. He was happy to find the coil of rope was still around his shoulder and quickly tied off the dish onto the railing. He made sure it couldn't move again.

two **GILLY**

NELSON TURNED HIS attention back to the boat making its way through the storm. In just a few minutes it would be tying up at his dock. Nelson had to wonder who this person was. It couldn't be any of his guides. All of them were a little crazy, but none would ever think of being out on the water today.

At the bottom of the walkway that connected the front deck to the docks was the boathouse. Nelson stepped in to grab a towel. He came back outside with it around his neck, a bright striped thing that must have been left by some yachters. It kept his neck warm and stopped the cold water from trickling down the collar of the yellow bathrobe. If he looked ridiculous, he didn't care.

The boat approaching was very much like any of the ones used by the guides. It had two chairs for guests amidships and a seat in the stern within comfortable reach of the long tiller arm connected to the outboard engine. Nelson watched as the skipper deftly steered while working with the gusting wind to manoeuvre the boat onto the moorage. The skipper waited patiently for just the right moment, then threw the motor into reverse and stopped the boat as it kissed up against the wood.

The skipper leapt out of the stern seat, moving quickly to the side of the boat. They reached down to pull out a short tie-up rope that ended in a carabiner, a strong metal clip used by climbers. They waited, judging the heaving of the boat as the waves pushed it into the docks. As the boat rose and the gunnel came past the tie-up rail, the skipper flicked the rope through the gap between the rail and the dock and clipped it onto itself. The boat continued to rise past the rail and the skipper stepped off. Tying up the boat and getting out of it was all accomplished in one smooth motion.

Whoever this was, they had obviously spent some time on the water. Nelson had never seen a carabiner used on a tie-up rope. He ruled out most of the regular guides in the area, mainly on account of the weather. And now he noticed something else that removed the other guides as choices. This skipper was decidedly female. Even under the bulky survival suit, it was unmistakable.

Then she turned and looked at Nelson. She had eyes like a Cooper's hawk.

For Nelson it was like being hit in the chest. He let out an "oof" and immediately hoped she hadn't heard it. It sounded like he had just called her an egg if he was speaking French. Nelson could only stand there. He became strangely self-conscious. He suddenly began to care what he looked like. His outfit was ridiculous. He knew he had to say something, anything.

"Kind of a windy day to be out on the water." Even to himself he sounded like someone's father.

"Yeah, the air is really fresh though, eh? Makes you feel like spring is almost here."

Spring? This makes her think of spring? Nelson was a little dumbfounded. He stood there gaping like a fish. There was an awkward pause you could drive a barge through.

The visitor finally spoke up.

"Hey," she said, extending her hand. "My name is Gillian, but most people just call me Gilly. Are you Nelson?"

The question made Nelson remember Vop's robe had the initials "IV" prominently sown onto the left breast.

"Um, yeah, I'm Nelson, though I guess you must be wondering about the initials."

Nelson self-consciously touched the embroidery. He realized she wasn't even looking at it and probably hadn't even noticed. "The robe, it belongs to one of the other guides." He felt compelled to continue explaining himself. "We were having a hot tub party the other night—well, it wasn't just him and me, I mean, there were some other people here as well, and you know, stuff, uh, stuff gets left behind."

Nelson could feel himself reddening. His ears grew alarmingly warm.

The woman simply stood there quietly, a slight smile on her face. He was blurting out the answers to questions that she hadn't even asked.

Gilly spoke up again before the pause got too awkward. "Oh, no, no. I understand. I've heard about some of the guide parties up here. No need to explain."

"Say," Nelson said, seeing an opening. "I'm dealing with a little situation up on the front deck. Do you think you could give me a hand for a few minutes?"

three **THE PALANTIR STONE**

WITH TWO PEOPLE, and the cooperation of the wind, getting the satellite dish back to its original position and pointed in the right direction was quickly accomplished. Nelson made sure the lag bolts were actually inserted in the holes this time and then tightened down. They were finished and back inside the resort before it began to rain and blow again.

"Wow, that's a huge TV!"

"It's thirty-two inches from corner to corner. Herbert, the owner, had to get the biggest one he could find," said Nelson. He sounded a little envious. Not of the television, perhaps, but of the ability to just go out and buy this whole setup.

The TV took up space in the room like an important piece of the furniture. At the moment, though, it was no more than an awkward coffee table.

"So the guy who owns this place just dumped all this here for you to sort out?" Gilly asked, sounding incredulous. It did seem a bit haphazard.

"I wish it was even that organized," said Nelson. "If he had just left it for me, at least I would know where we were. He and his buddies left here thinking they had actually set up a satellite TV system. I have no idea what they did—or what they didn't do."

"Wishful thinkers?"

"Just so you know who we're dealing with, see that, um, trophy over there on the shelf?"

Nelson pointed to an odd pile of airplane parts—a broken piston, a piece of throttle control, and a couple of cracked spark plugs—spray-painted gold and mounted on a black wooden base.

"Herbert has two brothers. They all own float planes and spend quite a bit of time flying from here to Seattle and up into the inlets. At the end of each summer that trophy gets awarded to the brother who had the most extreme screw-up while in the air. That throttle control is the one that fell off into Herbert's hand while he was coming in for a landing out in front of the resort."

Nelson tried to turn on the television but the screen remained dark.

"Looks like we may have to try and realign the dish toward the satellite or something. There's no signal coming in."

Nelson felt peevish about the whole situation. He was talking to himself more than anyone else. Gillian walked around the TV console the way she might view an important sculpture in an art gallery.

"It looks like it's all teak on the cabinets." She paused for a moment, looking down at the jumble of wires. The lights on the two metal boxes blinked on and off implacably.

"Um, I'm no expert, you know, but shouldn't this box be plugged into the other box beside it? This cord is just coiled up here."

She held up the end of the cord in question. It had a complicated connector that looked like it would match an equally complicated receptacle. Nelson stared at it, open-mouthed. He took the cord from her hand and plugged it in. He tried turning the TV on again. There was an encouraging noise and some lines appeared on the screen. After a flicker, an image suddenly appeared. The sound of an excited announcer's voice filled the room.

The two of them looked down at what they had accomplished.

It was a fashion show. The host gushed about the brilliance of the designer and how wonderful it was to be there in Milan witnessing such genius. The models had short, mannish haircuts and wore slacks and blazers under big overcoats with even bigger shoulders. The tall, thin women filled the huge screen, flouncing down the walkway as if they were doing the most important yet boring thing in the world. Nelson and Gilly stood motionless in rapt attention. Their sodden clothing dripped water on the floor.

Television had arrived at Stuart Island, and Nelson and Gilly were suddenly dropped into the front row, actually in the audience. Nothing they were wearing would be appearing on the runways of Europe anytime soon. Gilly unconsciously plucked away a small leaf stuck to her cheek by the wind and rain. The wind had picked up again and rain ran in rivulets down the windows. These distant images that had magically appeared in the storm-darkened room had their audience mesmerized.

four **HOW TO CLEAN A FISH**

NELSON WILLED HIMSELF back into consciousness. It felt like he was waking up in the back of his guide boat with no sense of how long he had been asleep. He hoped Gilly hadn't noticed.

"So, I guess you're here about working shore staff this summer?" he managed to say.

Gilly looked up, a little startled.

"Well, actually…" She struggled to find the right words. "I was hoping to use my boat and, you know, do some guiding."

Nelson was taken a little aback; this was proving to be a morning of firsts. He had just fired up the first TV in the area and now this, a woman asking for guiding hours. As far as he knew, there had never been a female guide before, certainly not in the rapids and probably not on the whole coast of BC.

"Uh, you're looking to take people fishing?

"That's usually the way it works, eh? You need someone to hold the rods and, you know, pay money to do that."

"It's just, umm…" Nelson was acutely aware of those eyes watching him. "Uh, there's a lot to it. I mean, you have to be able to catch fish, to start with."

Gilly seemed to have been waiting for him to mention this. She looked at him with a slightly mocking smile.

"Speaking of which," she said, "is it okay if I use your water and cleaning table down on the dock? I've got a couple of fish in the box that need cleaning."

"You were fishing on the way here?" Nelson didn't add "on a day like today," but he was certainly thinking it. What kind of fish could she possibly be talking about?

"Well, sure, I can, uh, turn the water on for you." Nelson was more curious than anything else.

They headed back outside into a gale-force wind. Nelson, acutely aware he was still wearing a bathrobe, was glad for the towel he had managed to grab. He tied up his regained belt and clutched the towel about his throat protectively as he trailed after Gilly. She hopped on board her boat nimbly despite the way it heaved up and down, pulling on the tie-up rope.

She reached into the fish box. Her back was to Nelson so he couldn't see what was inside. The next thing he knew, two beautiful spring salmon lay shining on the dock like two pieces of polished silver against the rough boards.

"Whoa, those are a couple of nice fish." Nelson didn't usually comment on fish quite so enthusiastically, but he couldn't help himself. He didn't really know what he had been expecting. Anyone would be pleased to bring these to the dock, and hard enough for one person in good weather.

Gilly didn't pay him any attention. She flipped the first fish up onto the cleaning table. A quick swipe of her blade and she opened the stomach cavity of the first one, from the anal vent to just below the chin. Another quick motion of her knife and the entrails hit the water, much to the delight of a surprised seal. With one hand she held the fish and with her other hand she flipped the knife end for end in the air and caught it. There was a spoon-shaped piece of metal on that end for cleaning out the top of the cavity. A few scrapes of the spoon and all the blood and the lone kidney also hit the water. She changed her hold. Two more semicircles with the razor-sharp knife around the gills and they were gone, one fish done. The second fish was cleaned in the same manner. Then she washed down the fish and the cleaning table with the hose.

Nelson watched quietly. She had obviously done this before a couple of times. Some of the guys who worked for him weren't that fast. He couldn't help himself. He had to know.

"So, where did you catch these, anyway?"

Gilly flashed him a large smile. Again, it was like she had been waiting.

"I don't usually give away my fishing secrets." She was teasing him now. "But I guess if I was working here, I'd have to share some of that information, wouldn't I?"

Nelson had to admit she had him there. He had opened that door and she had simply walked through it.

"Yeah, I'd still have to give that some thought. I know some of our guests would think I was sending them out with a cabin girl or something—uh, no offense. Listen, why don't I show you where you can stay for the night. All the cabins are empty. You can choose for yourself. There's plenty of food for dinner. Maybe we can talk some more in the morning?"

"Aw, that's really generous of you. I'd love to stay here— you know, take you up on such a wonderful offer, eh." Gilly sounded a little wistful. "I mean the lodge is amazing and all but... No... I have to go pick up my kid."

"You have to, uh, you have to... Say what now?" Nelson couldn't quite understand what he was hearing. Was she actually planning to go back out in this?

"My son. He'll be getting out of school in another couple of hours. You know, school's on Quadra, we live on Read. I have to go meet the school bus and pick him up."

Nelson looked out at the water. If anything, the conditions now were worse than earlier.

"You're trying to tell me that you're going back out in that?"

"Someone's got to be at the dock when the school bus gets there, or the little guy would be very sad. It's just to the government dock on the north end of Quadra. It's not like it's that far."

"Far" was a relative concept on the water. In the summer, with a light breeze, calm water, and sunshine, sure, the north end of Quadra was just a few minutes. But, on a day like today?

"You do this often?" Nelson was beginning to put the pieces together.

"Well, yeah." She shrugged.

And the reality dawned on Nelson.

"You do this all winter?"

"Yeah, every day there's school, anyway."

Nelson winced. He had his own experiences with boating in the winter.

"So you're heading back there now?"

Clearly she intended to do just that, but Nelson still couldn't quite wrap his head around the idea.

"Don't you want to wait until the wind backs off or the rain stops, or something?

"Oh, no, it's fine. The school bus has to keep to the schedule."

Nelson looked at her and noticed some things. For instance, she really wasn't very big. The bulk of the survival suit hid her slight figure. Her size had more to do with the force of her personality. He also noticed a small brown curl poking out from under the drawstring hood of the survival suit.

"How many days of school are there?"

"Oh, maybe a couple hundred. But don't worry; my son gets the summers off. There are plenty of times when I'm available to guide."

Nelson didn't know what to say. Of course there was a school bus. Forget what was happening on the water; she had to be there, like it was the most normal thing. It ran on its own schedule, you see!

He helped her load the perfectly sport-dressed fish back into the boat. A boat that was clean and tidy in a way that would put most of the guys to shame. He tried to help her untie, but her system was minimal. She had it done before he could even reach down. He watched as she manoeuvred her boat away from the dock. As she turned and headed out to open water, he yelled over the wind.

"You listen on 16?"

"Yeah, most of the time. I talk on 68."

"If you're okay being on standby, once the boat traffic starts showing up, we usually need extra guides."

"Great, I can be here."

Gilly flashed him another big smile and then she was gone. Nelson was left standing on the dock, wondering what the hell he had just done.

five TIME WARP

ABOUT THE SAME time Gilly was pulling away from the dock at Dent Island Lodge, I was pulling out of the weather into a small bay on Read Island. Tucked into a very sheltered spot in the bay was the float house of my friends, Carl and Stephanie. I had known them for a number of years, from before I started guiding. I always liked to drop by and get caught up on things. With the wind blowing a gale, I could find no good reason to continue on to Stuart Island, where the guiding season would begin soon enough. There was still plenty of time to get things ready; one more night away wouldn't matter.

The float house was what you might call "old school"; very similar to the one Vop and I shared on Stuart. Carl and Stephanie's had started life as a cabin at Manson's Landing. As the name implied, the Landing was a routine stop for the Union steamships when they still ran up the coast. People could rent the cabins and spend a week or two of summer vacation there.

All the cabins at the Landing had been sold off a few years back. Carl saw buying one as a bargain. He had it dragged onto a float made out of logs, a system often used to create float housing for logging camps on the coast. However, the logs eventually become waterlogged and the whole thing would start to sink lower and lower in the water. Carl had a plan for this eventuality. I found him surrounded by designs and drawings of what he wanted to do. He was only too happy to explain it all.

It involved hauling the house off the old float and onto the shore. Conveniently, there was a flat spot on top of a high bank near their moorage. The water there was quite deep. When the tide was just the right height, the float could be towed into place. The house would then sit level with the shore and could be winched off easily when the new float was ready for it.

Carl and a neighbour had already drilled a couple inch-and-a-half holes into the rock on the high beach, then bashed in a big staple. The plan was to fasten a big block pulley to that. Carl would attach a thousand feet of heavy-duty rope to the skid logs, thread it through the block, and then send it out to a tug. As the tug moved slowly away, the cabin should just trundle up onto the beach, almost by itself. The next phase of the project, assembling the new float, could be done in the deep water along the shore.

"It's going to be outstanding, man. A real state-of-the-art float. We're going to use ferroconcrete over a wire mesh to make individual chambers, each one with an access, so if any water does get in, it can be pumped out quickly."

Carl showed me the diagrams and lists of supplies he had meticulously compiled.

"We're going to assemble the float in the deep water at the base of the high bank. Each compartment will be made onshore, then floated over and filled with enough water to settle it into place. Once all the compartments are assembled and decked over, the water gets pumped out and we drop the house back on."

"You're going to drop it on?" I asked, not quite sure how that would be accomplished.

"A friend of ours has a seventy-foot floating crane. They use it to clean the nets on the salmon farms they are starting to build around here. It can lift this house up, no problem. The float is moved out, the crane comes in and picks up the house, the float is brought back in and the house is lowered onto it. Just as simple as that."

It certainly sounded simple enough. Carl kept brushing his long hair back with his left hand as he described the steps. It was a bit of a nervous tick, what you might call a "tell." It made me wonder.

Of course, paying for all this was not a problem. Carl had a successful summer last year, what with all the new guides being hired at the resorts. Carl was a grower. The plants that the RCMP had ripped up last summer belonged to him, but that was just a small part of his operation. In fact, he had grown those plants there on purpose, along the flight paths the police commonly used. If he let them feel like they were eradicating pot plants, then they had no reason to look further. Our conversation touched on his plans for growing as well.

"Did you get to try any of the stuff we grew last summer? That new method is giving great results." Carl was an early adopter of all kinds of new approaches. He had been working with some others down on Texada to create a hybrid plant designed to grow well in the local climate. One of his friends was an old draft dodger who had arrived from California with some seeds. These early plants had been crossed with some seeds brought back from Thailand and a new strain was developed. The result was so potent, someone named it Time Warp, and the guides lined up at his door.

Carl had never heard what happened to the plants that were confiscated by the RCMP. When I told him they had spontaneously combusted after being stored in the hot engine room of the RCMP boat, Carl had to hear all the details.

six THE KITCHEN SINK

GILLY ARRIVED BACK at Read early, with time to spare before she crossed over to Quadra to pick up her son. She pulled her boat up to the kitchen side of Carl and Stephanie's place to have a word with Stephanie.

"Hey, Gilly, come on in," Stephanie said as she greeted her at the door. "Keep your boots on, though. You'll need them."

Keeping gumboots on was a good idea. That part of the house was sinking the most. The cast iron cook stove and the cast iron airtight for heating were located in the kitchen, so it was the heaviest room. Water slopped up between the floorboards from time to time, wakes from passing boats or even just small waves from the wind. Stephanie's blind old beagle snuffled along the floor, looking for anything that might have fallen off the counter. Occasionally some water splashed up and the snuffling turned to more of a gargle.

"Yeah, it's really gotten worse since the last time I was here, eh?" said Gilly.

"I'm not holding my breath, but Carl finally agreed to replace the old log float. I think the water was finally getting to his study."

"Well, that's a start anyway." Gilly was always something of an optimist. "And, speaking of starts, you know that guy at the resort you told me about, Nelson? He said he'd keep me on standby and he might be able to give me some hours this summer."

"Oh, that's great. The way you catch fish, there should be no problem with getting work up there. It's just being able to deal with the people you get in your boat. You know they're going to have doubts about you being a woman. At least until you get a couple of nice ones in the fish box."

"I've got two in the boat right now. Do you still have any of the Time Warp from last summer's crop? I'd consider a trade—some of the new and improved Time Warp for one of them?"

"I do have some left," said Stephanie. "We have one of those airtight sealing appliances, like they use at the resorts to preserve the salmon. Works great to keep the dried weed fresh for a long time."

After a quick trip out to the boat for an inspection of the salmon, they reached a deal. One fish was definitely worth two lids of the best dried flowers. Stephanie unscrewed the lid of a can of rolling tobacco. She measured two lids of the best flowers into a bag.

"So, a new float," mused Gilly as she watched Stephanie do a final inspection of the preserved flowering tops. "That's going to be a lot of work. When do you think it's going to start? I mean, looks like now would be good."

Another wave slopped through the floor and the beagle sneezed wetly.

"There's still a lot of planning to do. There are just so many details you have to keep track of. Which reminds me—Hey, Carl! Carl, honey!" Stephanie yelled loud enough to be heard in the study, from which came a muffled reply.

"Did you get a chance to look at the pins we talked about? You know, the ones to hold the skid logs, underneath the house? Remember, we talked about whether or not the logs were pinned in place?"

She had to repeat herself a couple of times before she was understood.

Carl finally yelled back, "Dave's here. He's going to spend the night. I can check it out tomorrow when he's gone."

"Who's Dave?" asked Gilly. She knew most of the people who lived on Read.

"He's one of the independent guides up at Stuart. You'll meet him if you're going to be up there. He's a nice enough kind of guy, but you know, maybe a little pompous. Most of the younger guides call him Mr. Giblin."

seven **VOP RESCUES A STRAY**

A FEW DAYS earlier, Vop had arrived at the house he shared with me at Big Bay on Stuart Island. He wanted to get the house opened up and aired out after the long winter. Although he made his home at the north end of Cortes Island, it was just a little too far away for him to commute when the season began. He didn't mind the rent he had to pay to have a place right on Stuart Island. It was a tax write-off, for one thing. He also enjoyed being in Big Bay for the summer, which was, after all, the heart of the action. Quite often, just being handy and available allowed us both to pick up extra hours.

When he arrived, the sun was shining and the winds were light. It was the kind of warm spring weather he was hoping to enjoy. Vop was especially fond of crab, but conditions around the island were not ideal for them. They needed a flat, muddy ocean bottom, and it was mostly rock around Stuart Island. So Vop organized the kitchen somewhat, got the water system running, and opened all the windows to the breeze. Then he set out for Frederick Arm, just north of Dent Rapids. At the head of the Arm, the water was quite shallow and the bottom was the kind of mud perfect for crab.

Vop put on his diver's mask and snorkel. Then he laid down on the bow of his boat, with his head and shoulders over the edge and his face in the water. He used his fishnet to reach down to the bottom and pull himself along. If he saw a good-sized crab, he could just scoop it up.

He was soon lost in the search through the murky water, poling the boat along with the shaft of the net. He had a couple crabs in the boat and was looking for one more. All he could hear was the sound of his breathing through the snorkel.

As Vop worked along the shore at the head of the Arm, a strange apparition began to take shape in front of him. He propelled himself closer and realized this wasn't another crab. He was looking down at a pair of bare human feet. Then the top of his head came in contact with something soft.

Vop gasped and sucked in water around the snorkel's mouthpiece. He looked up, coughing and sputtering, into the blue eyes of a man who stood almost chest deep in the water. He appeared to be wearing only an old blue boat tarp, tied around his waist, a hole cut in it for his head. His hair and beard were scruffy and bedraggled.

As Vop gaped at him, the man turned his head to stare into the clear sky and began to speak quietly. Vop had to strain to hear him.

"Ah, snalla," the man said. "Jag ar valdigt kall och hungrig, valdigt hungrig."

Vop was puzzled. The words were definitely not English, but there was something familiar about them. Vop's grandparents came from Iceland and still spoke their native tongue. What the man was saying had something vaguely Icelandic-sounding about it. Unfortunately, Vop had never learned to speak the language himself. But then, *hungrig*, hungry, whatever this guy was trying to say... Vop only needed to look at the skinny legs and arms emerging from the rough canvas to know he was probably starving to death.

The man followed Vop as he pulled the boat up onto a small nearby beach. There he found a crude shelter, not much more than some cedar branches stacked against a fallen log. This guy had been been living there. Vop looked inside but saw no belongings or anything else to give him an idea of who this guy was, where he came from, or how he got there. There was no clothing and no camping gear. Vop had to wonder how the man had managed to survive at all.

Vop gestured to the boat, inviting the man to get in. It didn't take much persuasion, even with the language barrier. Vop settled him onto the floor of the boat and did his best to wrap him up with a spare raincoat and a couple of life jackets. He wanted to protect him from the cool air of the ride back to Stuart Island.

Once they reached the house, Vop, who knew enough not to feed a starving man too much, heated up some soup and gave him a light meal.

Vop took a bowl of soup for himself. As they ate, he tried to find out something about the man, like his name or if there was someone to notify. Communication wasn't easy.

Vop pointed to himself and said, "Vop. My name is Vop."

The man looked puzzled. Every time Vop said the name "Vop," the man flinched. Vop quickly realized that "Vop" wasn't much of a name in any language, so he tried something else.

"But you can call me Ivor. Ivor Vopnstrom."

At this, the man brightened considerably. He began speaking, very quietly and with no eye contact, but very fast. It was a gush of words, almost as if the man thought Vop and he could speak the same language. Vop, of course, couldn't understand a word.

"How do you like the soup? The soup is good," said Vop, smiling vigorously and holding up his spoon. The man just continued to mumble. He didn't acknowledge Vop's spoon. He sat rocking gently in his chair and finished his soup.

After eating, the man pointed to the couch in the living room. He put his hands together under his chin, the international gesture for "I need to go to sleep." Vop took him into the back room, where we had a spare bed for visitors. He made him comfortable with sheets and blankets, and the man fell immediately into a deep sleep.

While he was asleep, Vop called Campbell River. He had a very frustrating conversation with a social worker there. A strange man speaking a foreign language, one that sounded like Icelandic, living almost naked under a log in the middle of nowhere, turned out to be a little hard to explain. While he was describing the bright blue tunic made out of a boat cover that the man was wearing, even Vop realized that he was essentially telling the social worker he had found an elf. The social worker was quite skeptical. The more Vop persisted with the story, well, the crazier he sounded. The social worker ended up suggesting Vop might want to come in for some counselling.

Not giving up easily, Vop then called the float plane office. He actually managed to arrange a pick-up for the next morning. The dispatchers at the float plane company were more used to hearing strange stories from the outer islands. They even offered to see the man to the Campbell River Hospital emergency room.

The next morning, all the flights in and out of Stuart Island were cancelled due to the weather. The man was still sound asleep.

Eight **THE SHAPE OF THE ROLLER COASTER**

VOP WAS AT the dock to meet me when I finally made my way through the storm and into Big Bay. Being met by him was unusual enough. Then he did his best to explain the situation.

"Hey, Dave, I'm really glad to see you. There's, uh, there's been a development since we talked on the radio. I found some guy living under a fallen log up in Frederick Arm yesterday afternoon. He's... he's up in the house right now. He slept most of yesterday afternoon and evening and only woke up about half an hour ago. You might want to go in quietly."

As we entered, Vop's new buddy was sitting cross-legged on the floor of the living room. He appeared to be inspecting the round rust marks in the carpet left by the propane tanks. He traced the patterns with his fingers, his brow furrowed in deep concentration. The patterns might have been crop circles in the green shag, full of meaning. He ignored our polite small talk and we were left staring down at him awkwardly.

"He's wearing your Stan Smyl jersey," I said, for lack of anything better to offer.

"I let him go through the closet to find some clothes. He was naked except for an old boat cover he must have found floating around. I looked through the shelter he had put together, but he had nothing."

"Okay. Interesting wardrobe choices." Along with the jersey, he was sporting Vop's leather cowboy hat. The brim hid his eyes from us.

"Do you know his name or where he came from?"

"Nothing, man. There was no ID or wallet, no food, nothing. I don't think he even speaks English, or if he did, he's somehow forgotten."

"Have you gotten hold of anyone, like social services in Campbell River, or…?"

"I had a conversation with social services. It didn't go well."

"Yeah, I can imagine." Actually, I couldn't imagine how that conversation might have gone. "But Vop, just because you found him doesn't mean you can keep him!"

"I know that. I talked to the float plane office and they'll see he gets to the hospital, at least as soon as the weather allows. Oh, hey, I almost forgot, I have a couple of crabs in my fish box. There's enough there for an appetizer."

Maybe we weren't being as excited about Vop's "development" as we should have been. But at least the guy was safe and warm, and we had two boatloads full of food for the three of us. The reality was, until the weather backed off and we could get him to town, he was in the best place he could be.

It wasn't like this had never happened before. There was something about the wilds of British Columbia that attracted a certain kind of traveller. I had been in a tree planting camp a few years back. A couple hundred miles from the nearest town and another guy just showed up. He accepted some food and a place to sleep for a day or two, but insisted that he was just "out for a walk" and left to continue with it.

Many of my friends read *The Eden Express: A Memoir of Insanity*, by Mark Vonnegut, when it first came out. I knew several of them had also come across lost people like we had. Sometimes the outcome was much more tragic. The lessons in the book added to the understanding we could bring to these situations. As I watched our friend trace the rust circles in the carpet, a line in the foreword written by the author's father came to mind: "His wish is to tell people who are going insane something about the shape of the roller coaster they are on."

nine **ON THE NATURE OF ART**

WINDSTORM OR NO windstorm, Vop and I still had to take care of business. As independent guides, we each made the rounds to the various resorts to arrange guiding hours. A single excursion like that could give us bookings until the end of the summer, but the sooner we did it the better. The problem was it meant leaving "Stan the Steamer," as we had taken to calling Vop's rescue (he seemed to want to keep his namesake's jersey), alone for the day. We were both concerned about leaving him unsupervised, but Vop hit on a very elegant solution. He remembered that Stan had been very excited when he saw the boxes of oil pastels that I kept in the spare room. Stan had pointed and even spoke—or at least, mumbled in his own language—a rare occurrence: "…farger, farger, det fanns sa manga farger…"

I got the pastels and some paper out and settled him into the spare room. By the time Vop and I left, he was happily making marks on the paper. We promised each other to get the visiting done as quickly as we could. It was similar to leaving a young child at home. We didn't trust leaving Stan alone to his own devices.

Of course, hurrying was easier said than done. Just showing up, booking in a few dates, then leaving would have been considered bad manners. There was all that catching up to do. Each stop was more of the same. Births, deaths, marriages, and trips to exotic places—many things can happen over the course of a winter.

Vop and I arrived back at the same time, but it was getting late in the day. We were both hungry and a little afraid of what we might find inside the house. However, as it turned out, we had nothing to worry about. We found Stan still in the spare room. He had run out of the paper I had given him and had started in on covering a stack of old newspapers.

The spare room was adjacent to the woodshed, which housed some of the firewood and kindling, as well as newspapers used to start up the wood stove. There was now newspaper all over the room, each sheet carefully coloured in. Stan had blocked out the text in one colour, pictures in another, and he had worked his way through the whole pile. He had then turned to the firewood and had traced the grain of the wood using different colours to accentuate the changing shapes. Even the kindling had been treated in the same fashion. The level of detail and workmanship was incredible to see.

The storm eventually backed off and the plane finally arrived. By that time, what with all the food and warmth and engagement on his task, Stan was quite docile. We loaded him on the float plane with no trouble at all.

A few days later, I found Vop standing in front of the woodstove, holding one of the hand-coloured pieces of firewood. He was turning it over and looking at the way the grain had been outlined and traced in different colours.

He finally looked up and said to me, "So, Dave, you're an artist. Do you think it's okay to burn this stuff, or is it, you know, like art now?"

ten OFFERINGS

ONE OF THE small tasks we did to prepare for what was shaping up to be a busy season was to gas up all the spare gas tanks. It was so much easier to have a few tanks ready to go and to be able to switch them out as needed. As I pulled my boat into the gas dock, I noticed that Troutbreath had been busy over the winter. On one side of the boatshed, he had built a smaller room where he had set up a kind of store. He was only too happy to take me through and show me the results of his labours.

This winter he had been invited to meet up with a yacht in Fiji. The owners, who had spent several summers docked at Big Bay, took a special interest in Troutbreath. During Troutbreath's trip to Fiji, the dive master, employed by the owners of the yacht, had taught him how to dive. The yacht owners had even set him up with some basic equipment, enough that he could spend time underwater when he returned to Stuart Island.

"You remember Lars and Gunnar?" Troutbreath asked. They were the sons of the family who had taken Troutbreath to Fiji.

"I think I might have met them once or twice with you at the Wheelhouse Pub."

"They're going to bring the yacht up here again a few times this summer. We'll have to get together over a beer at the pub sometime. Lars and Gunnar are doing some very interesting research. They've been looking into the legends and oral histories of the Indigenous People from around here."

"They must have had so much knowledge and understanding. So much that has been lost."

"Yeah, I know. You guys would have lots to talk about. Anyway, it's a little trickier diving here than it was in Fiji," Troutbreath continued. "It's not just that the water is colder, of course, but you don't realize how strong the currents are here, even on a small tide. You can only be down there for a half hour or so after slack before you start getting pushed around pretty hard. But it was all worth it. You wouldn't believe how much is on the bottom. I mean, I knew that I'd find something, but it's exceeded my wildest expectations. It's like an archeological exploration in one of those cenotes in Mexico where they made sacrifices to the gods."

Troutbreath housed these finds in his new store. He had top-of-the-line rods, reels, fishing nets, and even tackle boxes still full of fishing necessities. And sunglasses. Pair upon pair of sunglasses.

"I'm just getting started, really. I set up a grid system and I'm working through different layers. The sunglasses help me date the layers. Because I can only be down a short time, progress is slow, but you can see why I want to do it. Most of this stuff is brand new, and after a little cleaning and some oil, it's ready to go. There are Fenwick rods, and Penn and Ambassadeur reels. I mean, it's like it has all rained down from above. But here, let me show you my best find so far."

Troutbreath opened up a drawer beneath a display table. He pulled out a small, water-stained presentation case. I recognized the logo on the outside, and sure enough, inside was a very expensive Rolex Oyster watch.

"Are you serious? Someone lost this over the side of their boat?"

Troutbreath slipped the watch onto his wrist and admired it. Any sign of the time it had spent on the bottom had cleaned off easily. The case was a little worse for being submerged, but this was still a working and very desirable timepiece.

"Have you tried to find the owner?" I asked. "I should think they'd want to get it back."

"Oh, I'm pretty sure the owner doesn't want this back."

"How can you say that with such certainty?"

Troutbreath smiled. He took the watch off and handed it to me. "Here. It's inscribed."

I turned the watch over, and sure enough, there on the back was a very finely engraved inscription:

TO

THE LYINGEST

CHEATINGEST

UGLIEST

SON OF A BITCH

FROM

HIS WIFE

eleven **A MIGHTY HUNTER**

IT WAS GOING to be a busy summer. It was also starting to look like it was going to be one of those summers where, no matter how hard you try, things just keep going sideways all on their own. Not just for the guides, either. Mr. Carrington, the owner of Big Bay Marina, felt that way as soon as he rounded the back of the resort's restaurant and saw what was going on at the back door of the kitchen.

There were a number of things Mr. Carrington cherished about his resort. Near the top of this list were the deer that came down to his front lawn. They were Stuart Island deer, born and raised, and they never left. They didn't grow very big; the mature bucks were about the size of a golden retriever, but with horns. Mr. Carrington held them in the same regard as some people did for that breed of dog. He let them wander the lawn and didn't mind them eating the apples that fell off the trees. His guests were always out taking pictures of them. Given the comments he received, he was convinced that a few fallen apples were a fair trade for such an asset. And Mr. Carrington had names for all of them.

As he walked around the back of the kitchen, he found the new cook he had hired standing in the back doorway. He was holding a double-barrelled shotgun with a whole iceberg lettuce jammed onto the end of the barrels and was using this to feed "Lady," the favourite and most venerable matriarch of the deer herd.

As far as Mr. Carrington was concerned, this was the daytime equivalent of pit lamping. Not only was it a highly unethical method of hunting deer, the shotgun was pointed at Lady the Untouchable.

The cook was already on probation. One of his duties was to feed the resort guides, and they were not very happy— a bad sign this early in the season. A few days ago the cook had served them hotdogs for lunch without removing the plastic wrappers. You could still see the maker's trademark. A couple of the guides had written a song about "wieners you could read."

Unrest among the guides, and now this. The cook found himself on the next available plane back to town. A plane that he shared with just one other person: a strange-looking fellow who appeared to be hiding from view behind a leather cowboy hat.

Fortunately, Mrs. Carrington had just opened a query letter from a gentleman who had been in Big Bay last summer. He was there as a chef on one of the luxury yachts moored at the Big Bay docks, he had enjoyed being in the area so much, and he wanted to return. She had sampled the man's creations and thought he would be just what the resort needed to keep pace with the changing times. Big Bay was becoming less of a fish camp and more of a destination that lived up to the idea of a resort.

twelve **THE TROUBLE WITH BEING THE GO-TO GUY**

WORD OF THE new hand at Big Bay's kitchen quickly spread. The place was open to the public, and the public included guides, as long as they were reasonably presentable. I took the earliest opportunity to try out the new menu. It was time for spending some of my tip money. It was true what they said: the man was a master, and the food well worth the slightly higher prices. The dining room was filled with people from the yachts as well as fly-in guests.

I was on my way back down to my boat when a guest from one of the yachts approached me. Double Double must have been talking about me at the Seattle Yacht Club. Double Double was the nickname of one of my long-time clients. Last summer I had helped him acquire some of the locally grown weed. He was entertaining an old college buddy and had asked for a favour. It was easy enough to accomplish and no need for much fanfare. Over the winter, stories of my discretion must have circulated. Apparently, I had become the go-to guy. If there was anything you needed while staying in Big Bay, Dave was the guy. The idea that I was opening myself up to other requests did cross my mind. I wasn't quite prepared for the kind of request I was about to encounter.

"Hey, are you Dave?" The man before me was talking in a whisper as if he didn't want to be overheard. Out of curiosity as much as anything else, I admitted to being Dave.

"Come on over here," he said. "I don't want my wife to see us."

These guys all seemed to live in abject fear that their wives might find them out. He led us down a finger float into a darker part of the moorage. The white hulls loomed over us like the adobe walls of a Mexican back alley. The guy was furtive and a little twitchy. He kept looking back the way we came. I was beginning to feel like I was back on the streets of Culiacán.

"Listen, Dave," he said, still whispering. "I hear you're the go-to guy in Big Bay if, you know, there's anything a guy needs."

The suspense was building. It was like he was trying to share a dark part of his soul and needed to summon up the courage to face it. He finally managed to put it in words.

"Do you think, do you think you could, ah, find me a ... a newspaper?"

The guy's dirty little secret was out. All cards lay on the table. It quickly dawned on me what this was about. Most of these guys had investments of some kind, some of them very time sensitive. Here he was, out in the middle of nowhere, no phones or newspapers, especially no business section with the daily stock market updates. I thought about the rather colourful but very old ones back at the house, but obviously those would be no help whatsoever.

"Sorry, but we don't get the paper up—"

I didn't get to finish my apology. The voice of a woman cut through the night.

"Henry Lawrence! I know what you're doing down there! This is supposed to be a vacation! Can't you just leave your damn stock market alone just for once? Get back up here right now and stop harassing all the guides. I'm sorry, young man, if my husband is bothering you!"

The way she said "stock market" made it sound like the word "mistress."

thirteen **THE LOW FLOATER**

THE WIVES WERE beginning to make their presence known. In the early days, fishing at Stuart Island was not a big attraction for them. Of course, there were always a few who enjoyed the outdoor experience, but they were unusual. As the boats got bigger and more comfortable and the cabins became more than bunkhouses for men who spent all their time on the water, more and more of the wives began to appear.

The increase in the number of wives helped Gilly achieve her goal of employment as a guide. There wasn't much to do for a customer's wife, lounging in a yacht tied up at the docks or sitting around in one of the cabins. Why not get a little fresh air, go out in a guide boat, and see some scenery? You could enjoy a beverage or two and share some stories with a friend. If you caught a few fish while you were doing all that, so much the better, especially if your husband didn't catch anything. Why shouldn't the guide be female? Gilly's boat was much cleaner and more organized. It even smelled better.

Gilly caught enough salmon, and the women enjoyed her company so much that she was being requested. Troutbreath and Nelson were both being asked if they could arrange for Gilly to take people out. The docks were so busy that even some of the husbands, the ones who saw the fish coming in, had asked if she was available. Nelson began using her just like any other guide.

Gilly was on her way from her home on Read to the Big Bay docks to pick up two guests very early one morning. The tide was flooding. Gilly was running against the water in the Yaculta Rapids just before Big Bay.

At the same time she was approaching Big Bay, the currents flowing out of it were pushing a low floater, a log that had rolled out from under a passing boom, past the point and into her path. Waterlogged and floating just below the surface, the log was extremely hard to see. The boom had rubbed off the rough outer bark, exposing the smooth inner bark. The log slipped through the water, leaving no ripples or other telltale signs of its presence.

With no warning, the bow of Gilly's boat ran right up onto the massive floater and she stopped dead in the water. She was almost thrown from her seat.

She gunned the engine, but the boat didn't move. She was just pushing her stern deeper into the water. She jumped up and ran to the bow and looked over. Her boat was completely stuck, hung up on the middle of the log. The log and her boat, with her in it, were now being pushed together down the rapids, like just another piece of debris.

Whirlpools were opening beside her. Currents were beginning to converge as she and the floater approached the middle of the channel, the dangerous spot where all the currents met in a great rush of water.

Trying to drive over the log was useless. Gilly realized that, as dangerous as it sounded, to go around the log, someone had to push the boat over to the end of the log. The only way to push the boat was to get out and actually stand on the log and push from there.

Gilly turned, carefully hanging on to whatever she could find on the bow, and lowered her feet onto the slick log. It was like trying to balance on a giant icicle. Her feet slipped so easily, there was no way she could stand up properly. Leaning on the small bow deck, Gilly tried pushing the log with her feet. As boat and log, a newly formed raft, rushed down the channel, she experimented. She found she could slide the log along and soon she and her boat were nearing one end.

Her foot slipped again. She was getting tired and she had to rest. She took a moment to see where she was. The water here was being churned into froth by the movement of the tide, the noise drowning out everything. The pressure ridge where the currents met was getting closer. For all that, she felt exhilarated, her body electric from the flood of adrenaline. Time stood still.

Gilly changed her position, hanging with her feet over the bow. She found another handhold that gave her more leverage. She got a new purchase on the log and was able to walk it along the bow and out into the channel. Suddenly, with one more step, the log was gone, whisked away by the current.

Gilly dragged herself across the bow and fell on to the floor of her boat. She stood and with a couple of quick steps was back in her seat. The motor was still idling. This time, when she gunned the engine, the boat leapt forward. She turned a little and tacked across the rip, using the force of the water to increase her speed. In a matter of moments, she arced across the point and into the quieter water of the bay.

Gilly noticed a couple of boats leaving the resort as she approached. Despite the obstacles, Gilly figured she was only late by about five minutes. However, the two guys on the dock did not look happy. She could hear one of them loudly complaining.

"That damn Carrington's set us up with one of the damn cabin girls! Hey, where the hell have you been?" he yelled to her as she approached. "Those goddamned other boats left half an hour ago."

"She was probably doing her hair, ain't that right?" his side-kick offered.

"Well, goddamn it, if we're going fishing, let's get going before there ain't any goddamn fish left," said the first man. They both climbed into the passenger seats.

Gilly had so much adrenaline still coursing through her, she could have snapped both their little pencil necks like so much dry kindling. She chose not to.

fourteen | **HECK**

LATER THAT MORNING I was waiting in my boat for another pair of Big Bay's customers. Troutbreath had warned me it wouldn't be an early start. I was taking out a man and his wife. Troutbreath thought the man was the kind of person who expected the fish to come to him. From that description alone, I identified my guests the moment they appeared on the walkway leading down to the docks.

As the man and his wife proceeded along the dock toward me, men from the surrounding yachts called after them. Well, they called out to the man, to be precise. The woman, who appeared to be much younger than the man, was largely ignored. The comments were as innocuous as possible, mostly just stating the obvious,

"Hey, Heck, you're going fishing?"

"Damn fine day for a boat ride!"

There was none of the usual exchange of insults or derogatory remarks. All the men showed Heck a solemn deference.

"The guy's name is Heck?" I'd asked Troutbreath. Troutbreath had organized things around this guy the day before. Originally, Lucky Petersen was going to be his guide. After Troutbreath met Heck he decided that sending the guy out with Lucky would end in disaster.

"He is Harvey 'Heck' Tydesco, some rich guy from the Midwest somewhere. He's supposed to have a ranch that's as big as a state, or it is a state—you know, another one of those guys. He's an important guy in agri-business. Apparently, his company, Tydesco Industries, is very 'vertically diversified.' They make a big deal about that in their prospectus. I always read up on new clients, as it helps to be forewarned."

"The prospectus? Really? How do you even find that stuff up here?"

"Oh, I have people in Seattle who look it up for me. You know, contacts. Anyway, Heck is used to getting his way, and it makes him hard to guide. He and Lucky have already met, and Lucky has begged off the assignment. You're my 'weird old guy' specialist." Troutbreath was only slightly joking. "So I swapped you two off."

Lucky Petersen didn't really care what anyone thought. And he certainly didn't mind telling the guests exactly what he thought of them. He would berate them for missing a strike, swear at them for losing a fish, or wave his fish club in their direction if they made a move toward tightening his drag. One client sat spinning the knob on his fishing reel. The poor man persisted even after Lucky had asked him to stop. Lucky finally stood up, walked to where the guy was sitting, took the rod and reel out of his hands, and pitched the whole thing into the water.

I didn't do things like that. I was calmer. Customer service skills sometimes won out over the ability to catch fish. The man approaching my boat was obviously used to being coddled. That's why Troutbreath had brought me in. It was, most of the time, a good arrangement for me. Guys like this kept me pretty busy over much of the summer.

After a leisurely walk down the dock, Heck and his wife finally arrived. Heck stood on the edge of the dock and looked my boat over. As he reached the stern, something in the water caught his eye.

"Hey, will ya look right down there," he exclaimed. "We don't need to go chasing around in some little runabout. There's fish right under the dock here."

Heck leaned over the water to get a better look. As he did so, a pair of sunglasses slipped out of his shirt pocket and splashed into the water, scaring away the fish.

"Damn it, did I just drop my goddamn Ray-Bans in the water?"

Heck looked down as the water swirled lazily over the spot where the Ray-Bans had disappeared. There was no hope of them coming back.

"Sweetheart," said Heck as he straightened up. "Can you go back to the boat and get me the spare ones? My hip is playing up a little today."

Heck's wife dutifully walked back to their yacht. Heck and I shared an uncomfortable silence while we waited for her. Without Heck, it didn't take her very long to return.

Heck helped his wife into the boat in a way that suggested he didn't need me to do it for him. She was much younger than Heck, perhaps by half. She wore diamond earrings and an expensive looking white gold and diamond bracelet. When Heck wasn't making her do things for him, he treated her like a delicate porcelain vase. He made a great deal of fuss with her seating arrangements. When he finally had her as comfortable as possible, he sat down beside her.

We made quick introductions. Then Heck's wife reached into the bag she was carrying and handed Heck a box of cigars, a box of fifty Roi-Tan Bankers. I knew them to be a small, cheap American cigar. I had to wonder at his choice. Most of these guys liked to smoke a cigar, but usually the more expensive variety. They all had a weakness for the Cubans.

Ever since the American embargo had been put in place, real Cuban cigars were hard to find in the United States. Canada had no such embargo. I could stop at any cigar store in Canada and still find real Cubans any time I wanted. I used this taste for fine but forbidden things to my advantage: I kept a box of them carefully stowed under the foredeck of my boat. Whenever someone caught a big spring salmon, I brought the cigars out to celebrate. I had a man out from New York City who caught a tyee. I still remember the look on his face when I opened the box of Romeo y Julietas in front of him.

"Man, you got a lot of class," he had enthused.

The cigars paid for themselves in no time.

Roi-Tan Bankers didn't really have the same kind of reputation—if you intended to smoke them, that is. As we pulled away from the dock and headed out to the fishing hole, he broke the seal on the new box and tucked a cigar into the corner of his mouth. He didn't light it, but by then the boat was running and it would have been impossible anyway. Looking back a short time later, I noticed that the cigar was beginning to disappear anyway.

By the time we reached the fishing hole, the entire cigar had disappeared. Heck had a huge wad in his cheek and he was working on it in a thoughtful way. As we stopped to get out the rods and start fishing, he leaned over the side to spit. Most of the cigar remains left the boat, but he wasn't all that accurate. Another cigar came out of the box and that too immediately began disappearing.

I put the wife's rod in a holder built into the gunnel of my boat. Heck held his with an air of gravity and importance.

When we had our lines baited and in the water, he had to lean over the side again. And spit. This time he put his finger in his cheek and dug around then spat again.

Heck cleared his throat and spoke to me for the first time.

"Say, Dave, ya care for a chew?"

I had been taken in by the same offer once. It was simple curiosity on my part. After all, how bad could it be? Chewing tobacco was basically tobacco leaves soaked in molasses. It was one of the worst things I have ever put in my mouth, an experience I never wanted to try again.

I gently turned Heck down. He looked disappointed. I sensed our conversation was going to become a balancing act. Now I needed to agree with him on something. Then he asked his next question.

"What's the altitude here, anyways?"

This wasn't the first time someone had asked this question. I had any number of ways to tell someone we sat at sea level. The degree of sarcasm depended on the rapport I had with the customer. With Heck, I carefully explained that we, indeed, floated on the ocean.

"Are you sure about that? This looks more like a lake, don't it?"

I had even heard that as a reply before. I didn't offer Heck a taste of the seawater. The way the cigars kept disappearing, I doubted he would have tasted the difference. I left the question alone. I knew from experience that guys like Heck never really cared about the answers once they had their minds made up.

I was pretty pleased with the way I was handling things. A guide was allowed to manhandle and verbally assault a guest if it meant getting a fish in the boat. That was acceptable in the heat of the moment. Anything else was strictly off limits. We never talked about religion or politics. Lifestyle choices, how much they drank or ate or chewed—it really wasn't our business. It might take years of guiding someone before some of these items ever became a subject of conversation.

Then Heck asked his next question. "I see Carrington's hired his self a n***** cook!"

The observation took me by surprise. The words hung out between us like a line of sour laundry. The casual racism was nothing new. I was used to it by now. Having blonde hair and blues eyes seemed to give some of my guests the idea I was a kindred spirit.

The other part of Heck's observation touched on something totally different, though. I was upset for the new chef. He was no mere cook. I had eaten his food. He was an artist, a real chef, and a true master of his craft. I had seen grown men eating in the restaurant with tears in their eyes.

His name was Babacar. He was well educated and spoke five languages. He had been Cordon Bleu–trained in Paris. His father was from Senegal and was a diplomat stationed there. His mother was from Indonesia, and his cooking was a blend of all those flavours. The guides were already calling him Baba.

Heck continued.

"He talks Frenchy and kinda cooks Frenchy-like, don't he? You like that stuff, Dave? It's all little bits of things. I have to order two meals just to get full."

As if to accentuate the problem, he took out another cigar and popped it into his mouth.

"It's okay, Dave, I know what you like. You come by this evening. We're gonna have us a real barbecue. I'm cooking."

For perhaps the first time, I didn't know what to say to a customer. The best thing to do was pull up the lines and go somewhere, anywhere, just not sit there blinking at the man.

I took them to the other side of the inlet, which was about as far as I could run before I ran out of places to go fishing. As we put our lines in the water and settled the boat down to a nice troll, Heck stopped chewing. It was the first time he hadn't chewed since he got in the boat. He finally turned to me and asked another one of his questions.

"Y'all have a marijuana problem up here, Dave?"

To this day I still don't quite understand my immediate response. Perhaps it was because we had passed Carl's boat along the shore. He was obviously tending to the year's new crop and his marijuana was on my mind.

Whatever the reason, without missing a beat I said, "Hell no, Heck. That stuff just grows everywhere, absolutely no problem at all. Why do you think they call it weed?"

Heck actually stopped chewing again. He looked at me, and his eyes narrowed. By mocking him before we had established the proper understanding, I had overstepped some boundary. An awkward silence descended over the boat. We didn't talk much for the rest of the session.

Heck went back to chewing his cigars. Every once in a while he fired a suspicious look in my direction. He seemed to be trying to figure out what kind of person he was dealing with here.

By the time we returned for dinner, the box of cigars was empty. A splatter of brown stains covered the side and the floor of my boat. Heck made a great show of helping his wife out of the boat. She picked her way through all the brown stains with an air of much practice. After they left, it was all I could do to put the engine in gear and head over to the gas dock. I felt a little queasy.

"Dude, you don't look so good. You're not seasick, are you, Dave?"

Troutbreath was peering down at me with a great deal of concern. I had managed to make it over to the gas float to top up my tanks. By the time I got there, though, the full experience of watching a guy chew his way through a full box of cigars was settling over me.

"You're kind of green. You need to barf?" asked Troutbreath helpfully.

"Oh, no thanks. I already did that on the way over here." I pointed weakly back the way I had come. "I just watched our friend Heck chew his way through a full box of cigars in four hours."

"Yeah," admitted Troutbreath. "I probably should have warned you. Heck is kind of a difficult customer, for sure."

"Difficult? The guy's a Confederate-flag-waving racist with an unsavoury tobacco habit. It was all I could do to remain civil. Even so, I may have said some things." My voice trailed off.

"That's not like you."

"I'm afraid Heck pushed a button. He's the kind of guy who would put ketchup on Baba's beef Wellington!"

I could tell by the look on his face I had pushed one of Troutbreath's buttons.

"Well, he is up here more for business than the fishing. He doesn't like to leave the comfort of his yacht often. So I haven't pushed the fishing idea that much. He certainly doesn't know that he can request the guide he wants. I'll just circulate him between you and some of the resort rookies. Hey, listen, are you going home or having dinner here?"

"Uh, yeah, no. Heck already invited me to the barbecue. But I think I've lost the stomach for eating anything."

"Let me suggest you find your stomach, man. Baba is still preparing a full menu for the restaurant."

"I don't quite understand. Why would he do that if no one is eating there?"

"It's all part of their fly-in package and it's already paid for. Mr. Carrington has an obligation, according to the small print in the brochure, to provide three meals a day. Mrs. Carrington is making him take it seriously. Mainly because she wants to enjoy Baba's cooking too. Someone's going to have to eat all the food Baba is making and that's going to be the guides. Mrs. Carrington is joining us and I'm breaking out a couple bottles of the good stuff. This summer has already been too busy, man. We need to do this."

If Troutbreath thought I needed to experience a three-course dinner prepared by a master chef, who was I to argue?

fifteen **THE HELPING HAND**

IT DIDN'T TAKE long for Mr. Carrington's vague apprehensions about what the summer had in store to become real. Losing the cook was one thing and it had been fairly easy to find a replacement. Baba was extremely popular with a certain kind of client and he added another level of refinement to what the resort could offer. Things actually worked out very much for the better.

Mr. Carrington was able to find a little optimism. It was short-lived, however.

That night, on Heck's yacht, after they had finished eating the barbecue, Heck pulled him aside.

"Say, Carrington, it's a real nice place ya got here. All the boys are enjoying theirselves. I want you to know I'll be bringing in some of my business associates. We'll have to talk about reservations and such, and there'll be a lot of 'em. I know you'll be able to take care of us, though.

"You know, it must be tough, all the work to keep things running. I was thinking I could help you out. I could bring up some of my Mexicans and we can spruce things up for ya— you know, jazz the place up a little. Make it more like what my boys are used to."

Mr. Carrington nervously pulled a couple of wood shavings from his coveralls. He didn't really trust Heck's taste in jazz. He asked what Heck might have in mind.

"Oh, not much more than a few cans of white paint. You'll barely notice any difference. What do ya say?"

A few cans of white paint, wondered Mr. Carrington. What did Heck want to paint? Then Mr. Carrington realized that everything Heck owned was white. His boat was completely white, the helicopter on its back deck was white, and Mrs. Heck wore nothing but white outfits. Mr. Carrington needed a little time to sort this one out.

He said the best thing he could. "Well, I'll talk it over with Mrs. Carrington, see what she thinks."

After asking around the resort the next day, Mr. Carrington's worst fears were confirmed by Heck's ranch foreman, who was enjoying a fishing trip for his labours. The foreman told Mr. Carrington that all of Heck's properties were painted white. All the houses and outbuildings—the barns, horse sheds, and workshops—were painted white. The fences were all white, as well as any rocks that might appear above ground. The tree trunks up to about twenty feet above ground were all white. In fact, almost anything that didn't move was treated to a coat of white paint. The foreman figured a little place like the resort could be done in less than a week.

Mr. Carrington disappeared into the boatshed and was not seen or heard from for several days.

sixteen **THE BLIND BEAGLE**

IT'S IMPRESSIVE HOW much food two guides can eat, especially when things are busy. Even with free meals here and there, supplies had to be replenished on a regular basis, every two weeks. With the amount of work and the general busyness of starting up for the season, two weeks went by quite quickly. Of course, the only place for that kind of shopping was Campbell River.

It meant a trip first by boat to Heriot Bay on Quadra Island, where we had our cars parked. A government dock there provided us with a safe tie-up spot for the boats. We'd switch over to one of the cars and drive to the ferry on the other side of Quadra. A short ferry ride and we'd be disgorged in downtown Campbell River. The sudden exposure to that many cars and people was consistently disorienting.

I was happy to get away for the day. This would be just a regular shopping run, and Vop didn't need to accompany me. I even had time to make a short detour by Read Island. I was very curious to see how things were coming along at Carl and Stephanie's float house. A visit there always included a little shopping anyway.

I found Carl sitting at the kitchen table, which he had cleared to make way for a project. He had made a model of the new float out of blue Styrofoam and Popsicle sticks. Discarded chunks of Styrofoam and pieces of Popsicle sticks lay where they fell. The old house and the old float were recreated in a similar fashion. Carl had carved remarkably accurate cedar logs out of the Styrofoam and he'd added playing cards for the walls of the house. He'd found a kid's Meccano set in the thrift store and constructed a crane with it. He appeared ready to begin a scale model demonstration.

"Hey, man, come on in. You can leave your gumboots on." Carl was beginning to accept the reality of the "float" house. Despite his attention to detail on the model, none of his plans had yet to manifest beyond the kitchen table. "Let me show you what we've been doing."

Using his carefully assembled models, Carl showed me how everything was going to work. First he put the house up on a block of leftover Styrofoam, explaining that it was the high bank of the beach.

"The demonstration begins," he said, "after the house has been successfully moved into the bay at high tide and winched off the old float up onto the high bank."

Houses like this one were used in just such a manner at logging camps years ago. They sit on four logs stacked in a box shape designed for that purpose. Carl had even recreated the skid log system under the house out of the same blue foam. The model house sat proudly on the four model logs on the model shoreline.

"The old float will be towed away and the logs will be salvaged," he said. "Cut up for siding and rough building material. Our next-door neighbours have a mobile sawmill. When the new float is ready, the barge carrying the crane will first come alongside and pick up the house. Once in the air, the barge and the house will be moved out into the bay a bit." Carl moved the crane and house together away from the foam block shoreline and brought the model of the new float up beside the shoreline instead.

"Now the new float has been brought in. It has to be tied off to the land so it can't move unexpectedly. Then the crane will come back alongside and drop the house onto the new float."

He moved the crane and its float closer, then realized he hadn't provided for a way for the crane to actually pick up the house. We had to pause and smoke another joint while I watched him do some fiddling with string and another Popsicle stick to connect his Meccano crane to the model house. The harness, when he finished it, was a work of art. He attached it to the hook on the crane, picked up the house, and placed it gently on top of the new float.

"It's going to be beautiful, man. It will just be so slick. They use the crane to hoist nets and cables all covered in barnacles and stuff. They weigh thousands of pounds. It will lift the house no problem. It will be so smooth; we won't even have to move our stuff out. It can all just stay right here."

Carl ran his hand through his hair. One side was starting to stick up a little.

"Wait, you're going to leave everything still inside while you lift it?"

"Yeah. Stephanie's not crazy about the idea either, but moving everything out, it's just all kinds of work for no reason. We'll just have to move it all back inside again." Carl swiped the side of his head again.

I had to admit there was some logic to his reasoning. He and Stephanie continued to live in the float house while the new float was being built nearby. It would take days to dismantle everything inside. Just clearing out the kitchen alone, with all their canned goods neatly arranged in the pantry, the large bags of sugar and flour... It was an endless task. Then, if things went as expected, they would be moving it all back in again just a couple hours later.

"I'd say you've got it all pretty well worked out. You don't have any doubts?"

It was true; Carl did have it pretty well worked out. Who was I to argue with this kind of systematic planning? However, at the mention of the word "doubt," a cloud seemed to pass across his face. He sat looking at the house of cards and Popsicle sticks sitting on the new float. I suspected the choice of playing cards for a building material might have originated from some deeply subconscious place.

"No, no doubts. It's just that the last time you were here, Steph asked me something about the house and I can't remember what it was now. Oh well, never mind, it will come to me. Hey, can I roll ya a fatty for the trip to town?"

Just then the blind beagle, which had been snuffling around the kitchen, let out a satisfied snort, which was followed by the sound of crunching. Carl was probably looking for some kind of positive omen.

"Look at that," he declared. "Even a blind beagle can find a crunchy now and again."

seventeen

HOW I WON THE STUART ISLAND COMMUNITY SALMON DERBY

ANOTHER BIG REASON for the trip to town was the upcoming weekend. July 1 and July 4 were always significant days in the Stuart Island calendar. While June brought full docks and a full schedule of fly-in guests, the July 1 and July 4 weekend was the official start of summer.

July 1, Canada's birthday, didn't mean much to most of our American visitors. It was also the day the Stuart Island Community Association ran their biggest event of the year, the Stuart Island Community Salmon Derby. Of course, that didn't mean much to most of our visitors either. To be fair, this derby didn't have the biggest prize money. Actually, there was no prize money. No one would be counting crisp hundred dollar bills at the end of the day. There were no real prizes, either. No all-expenses-paid resort packages or even an engraved fishing reel. But neither did you have to pay any money to take part.

It was a pretty low-budget affair, and the winner wasn't going get rich. They did get a small, engraved plaque with their name on it, however, and it came with certain bragging rights. Those bragging rights, both for the guide and the lucky guest, were something of a higher order.

What set this derby apart is that anyone could participate. It was the only derby of the summer that included all the resorts as well as any locals who wanted to put a boat in the water. The official weigh-in was at the Big Bay Resort docks and was watched over carefully by Troutbreath, a man who was trusted by any and all, without reproach. It was the one derby that put all the guides in the area in competition with one another. They all took it very seriously. Winning this derby meant that, on this particular day anyway, you were the best of the best.

There was always a great deal of behind-the-scenes activity. The guides were all angling to get the best possible clients in their boat. You wouldn't want just any old stump sitting in the guest chair. You wanted someone who could pay attention and do what they were told. Preferably they would have been out with you before and were proven fish catchers, or at least proven fish winders. We could convince the guests they were the ones responsible for catching the fish. We did that on a regular basis. When it came time to weigh the fish at the end, though, we all knew it was the guide who really caught the salmon. The guest was just there to do all the tedious cranking and heavy lifting.

The evening before the big day, Vop and I sat at the kitchen table and tied our fishing leaders with special care. Vop shared some very strong opinions about the people he wanted in his guide boat. He had already talked with Troutbreath to make the arrangements. I, unfortunately, didn't have much choice in the matter. Mr. Breland had already requested my services.

Mr. Breland's regular guide from last summer, Wet Lenny, was now happily married to one of his daughters. Lenny had gone to work at Mr. Breland's company, where he proved to be a successful employee because of his well-known, organized approach to everything.

With Wet Lenny not guiding any more, Mr. Breland was reduced to using other guides. It gave me an opportunity to impress someone who could send a great deal of work my way. However, Mr. Breland wasn't exactly at the top of any guide's list as the perfect salmon-retrieval device.

When the day of the derby finally arrived, my chances of winning looked even worse. Mr. Breland didn't want to go out early, so I didn't pick him up until 9:00. Most of the serious participants had been out since dawn. When I arrived at the resort, he was alone. My chances of catching a fish were immediately cut in half. I had hoped his wife would be joining us. She was much better at the mechanics of catching fish than her husband, but I was denied even that advantage.

We started off in the Second Hole, but after about twenty minutes working our way through the crowds there, Mr. Breland suggested we go somewhere quieter so we could talk. We ran over to the other side of the Inlet. No one would disturb us there; all the smart money was expecting the winning fish to come out of First or Second Hole. On the way I tried to think what we could possibly have to discuss that was so important.

As expected, we were the only boat in sight. I set up a line and put some bait in the water, as much out of habit as from any prospect of catching something. Mr. Breland watched and waited until I was finished.

"So, Dave, you're probably wondering what this is all about. I appreciate you taking the time to talk to me." Mr. Breland was paying quite handsomely for our time alone, so I couldn't really object. "People tell me you're the guy to talk to. You seem to know just about everyone around here and not just at the resort.

"You might be aware that my wife's parents own a little property down there on Cortes Island. Now, they're getting on in years and they don't get up there as much as they used to. It's just not as easy for them as it once was. And us kids, well, we have our own families and the wherewithal to be up here on our own. Anyway, what I'm saying is they have decided it's time to sell the place. It's time for someone else to enjoy it as much as we did. I know other people are living in that house, though, and have been there for quite some time now. It's not that we resent them doing so. In fact, we appreciate how they have looked after things all this time. You know, just keeping the place heated over the winter and keeping the roof repaired has helped preserve it from the elements. Now, of course, whoever buys it, they are going to change all that. So, I'm hoping what you can do for me is put the word out. So these people can find somewhere else to go. We want them to have lots of warning, so they aren't left without anywhere to live."

Mr. Breland's instincts were correct. I was the guy to talk to all right. I had to admire him for wanting to do this. He had no obligation to tell anyone what his in-laws planned to do. In fact, I knew the cabin quite well. I had even stayed there a few times. It was where Vop lived the rest of the year.

Vop had found it years ago when he was a teenager roaming over Cortes Island. The beautiful log cabin had been there for years. Vop had returned to it often. Sometimes he would just hang out on the beach in front. Other times he might haul in some tools to repair the roof or replace window glass broken in a storm. Eventually, he ended up just moving in.

He took up residence there when guiding was done for the summer. Ownership had never really been discussed. Vop simply accepted its existence. He tended it, kept it warm in the winter, and made repairs as needed. If he thought about it at all, it was with deep affection. He saw it in terms of an overly large toadstool that had rooms and a cook stove.

By now it was his winter palace. I couldn't see him living anywhere else. Carol had joined him there last winter and had added her much-needed homey touches. The place now had curtains and sheets on the bed, simple things. It sounded like she had really enjoyed living there. She certainly liked the milder winter weather compared to the winters in the Interior. They would both find it hard to move on, and I was at a loss for words.

"Thanks for letting me know," I said. "I'm sure I know some people who can pass that along. I mean to, you know, to the people who need to know…"

I trailed off, feeling like Mr. Breland must see right through me.

At that very moment, a forty-six-and-a-half–pound spring salmon decided it was tired of living. Mr. Breland's rod went completely slack and the line suddenly began moving. Instead of trolling out behind us as the boat moved, it turned and ran the opposite direction. The fish caught up the slack line and the reel came alive. The line peeled out.

My instincts kicked in. I stood up and backed off the drag. I told Mr. Breland to stand up and turn in the direction of the salmon's run, but instead of heading straight, it turned back and started circling. It did two very fast runs around us and then headed for the boat.

I grabbed the net. The fish swam up, rolled over on its side, and allowed me to drop the net over its head. It wasn't until I tried lifting it into the boat that I realized just how big it was.

We both stood looking down at this thing for what seemed like forever. Finally, I said, "I appreciate your trust, telling me about the house. You can be sure whoever lives there will find out. Now, as your guide, I suggest we go weigh this fish."

Some nice fish were caught that day, but Mr. Breland's beat out the next biggest in the competition by twenty pounds.

I have watched other winners of the community derby. I have seen them get so excited they have simply walked off the docks and into the water. One guy was so caught up in the action, he spent the rest of the afternoon in wet clothes. His very expensive cashmere sweater stretched all the way to his knees, and he looked like he'd stolen a form-fitting dress from a flapper. It wasn't unheard for the winner to wake up in the morning on the resort's front lawn, a herd of deer cautiously grazing around them.

Mr. Breland was made of much sterner stuff. He hardly showed any emotion at all as Troutbreath and I hoisted the monster onto the scales. When Troutbreath announced the official weight, Mr. Breland just quietly said, "Wonderful, wonderful. It's a remarkable fish."

It could have been a fish caught by someone else entirely.

When Troutbreath asked him how he wanted his name to show up on the trophy, he had to think about it. After a long pause he said, "Just Doug... Just Doug Breland would be fine."

We told him about the party at the pub and the small award ceremony there, but he very politely declined the invitation.

"If you wanted to pick up the award for me, that would be just wonderful, wonderful. You could drop it off at the boat when it's convenient for you."

It was almost as if he found all the attention a little overwhelming. For someone so used to taking the centre of the stage, he was rendered strangely quiet.

eighteen

THE FOURTH OF JULY

THERE WAS NO trace of modesty at all when it came time for Heck Tydesco to celebrate his nation's birthday. Even if those celebrations were about to take place in a foreign country. The imaginary lines we call borders were exactly that: imaginary, simply a suggestion. Heck announced that he was going to throw the biggest birthday party the resort had ever seen and he was going to do the barbecue. Once again Troutbreath gave me the heads up to make sure I had dinner up in the restaurant.

I was guiding all that day, so by the time I'd putted over to the gas dock, I could hear the barbecue in full swing. The *Song of Joy* was tied up at the resort and Heck had somehow managed to talk the owner into deploying his cannon on shore. Guests were yelling back and forth. There were American flags everywhere, even one or two Confederate flags for good measure. The loud bang of the cannon being fired came like punctuation to it all. As I walked up to the barbecue pit, I smelled the black powder and the meat searing on the grates. The cannon fired once more.

"Heehaw," several people yelled. The clouds of smoke from the black powder drifted around them. A couple of them rushed through the haze to load the gun one more time.

I felt like I had stumbled into a reenactment of the American Civil War. A really bad one where the costumes are made out of Fortrel and polyester, and one or two participants sport a digital watch. Heck was presiding over the barbecue grills. He slopped red sauce out of a bucket over the slabs of beef with what looked like a two-and-a-half-inch house painting brush. A bottle of peach schnapps was being passed around.

Baba was watching the whole proceedings from a safe distance.

"Aye yi yi," he said to me as I took up a position beside him. "Bar, be, cue." He pointed with his chin toward the fire pit. It was pretty clear how Baba felt about Heck's approach to meal preparation. I happened to be in the kitchen the day the meat order for Heck's party arrived. Baba was especially astonished by the size of the monster ham steaks. Heck wanted to have the steaks fried up for breakfast, one for each of the guests. Baba didn't have any dinner plates big enough to serve them without the steaks hanging off the edge.

"Are you eating with us tonight?" he asked.

"I certainly am."

"Good," he said.

The scene in the restaurant was starkly contrasted to the one taking place outside. I walked through the main dining room, which was mostly empty. In the back was a separate room with a long table where the guides ate their meals. Today the long table was covered in a good tablecloth.

Troutbreath poured the wine. A reverent silence had settled over everyone, except for a quiet murmuring, as the guides admired the colour, clarity, and the thickness of the wine's "legs" as it ran down the sides of the glass.

Baba had prepared a choice of appetizer and a couple of salads, three main dishes, and a dessert and cheese plate to round out the meal. Troutbreath broke out a pound of caviar some especially grateful boat owner had given him. Baba served it with those little dollar-sized crepes and chopped boiled eggs.

Vop and Carol had a table to themselves near the kitchen, because Baba himself wanted to look after their meal. I hadn't been able to bring myself to tell Vop about the impending sale. It would have to wait until this evening was over. Then I would have to call a house meeting.

Meanwhile, the noises coming from the resort, all the yelling and yeehawing outside, seemed to recede farther into the distance.

nineteen **THE UNSINKABLE HERBERT CRANE**

HERBY HAD FLOWN in a couple of days after the July 4 celebrations. He usually spent the holiday at home, but we hadn't seen that much of him at all lately. On a visit to the post office to check mail, I stopped to see Nelson, who explained what Herbert had been up to.

Herbert's holdings now included a cruise ship business. He had purchased a retired Alaskan ferry. Over the winter he had it renovated at a boatyard in Seattle, upgrading the interior to make it much more luxurious, including the installation of a high-end galley. The idea was that people would drive on in their campers on their way up the coast. They could disembark anywhere there was a ferry dock, do some sightseeing and a little camping, and then meet the ship again. Nelson wasn't sure what kind of permission Herbert needed to use the BC Ferries docks, but Herbert said everything was in place. The maiden voyage was planned and a tentative date set.

"I have to warn you, though," added Nelson. "Herbert wants to outfit the new ship with several seventeen-foot runabouts like our guide boats, but fancier. He's brought one up here to try it out, see how well it works. You'll probably see him out there in it."

I didn't have to wait very long to see Herbert in action with the new seventeen-footer. Word had it the Nearside of the Arran Rapids was producing a few nice fish. The day after talking with Nelson I was there with a handful of other guides testing our luck. Not everyone liked to fish the Nearside. The rip could be very unpredictable and you had to pay close attention. The force of the water pouring through the rapids constantly shifted the line of forming whirlpools. One moment you could be safely in the back eddy, the next moment you were surrounded by vortexes opening all around you. The idea was to watch as the whirlpools formed and move farther into the calmer water as needed. On a big tide you might need to move well away from the danger. These were not the friendly, sleepy whirlpools that just happened to wake up at the wrong time, like the one that caught Wet Lenny. These were rabid dogs looking for a sign of weakness.

It was here of all places that Herby decided to join us and try out his fancy new guide boat. Similar to the First Hole, you had to follow an etiquette regarding where you placed yourself. Butting in was not polite. However, Herby was only moderately in charge of this boat. He hadn't quite mastered the controls yet and drifted in and out of the back eddy. He seemed oblivious to the water and how the tide was moving the rip line. Sometimes he drifted completely out into the main rapids before he motored back in and we had to move out of his way. I heard a couple of guides try to warn him about the whirlpools as the tide began to pick up.

"It's okay," he yelled back over the roar of the water. "This is a brand new Nantucket, and they can't sink."

Lucky Petersen's boat was next to mine, and he and I shared a glance, not sure if we had heard him correctly. I recognized the name. A Nantucket was the latest hull design from the east coast, a self-bailing hull made of foam sandwiched between fiberglass. An advertisement on the television showed one being shot up by a heavy-calibre machine gun. It continued to float as bullets tore away big chunks of it. As entertaining as the ad was, being shot up wasn't really the main the problem around here.

Lucky hit a fish and he and his boat disappeared down the tide. The new guide, Gilly, arrived to take a spot. She was alone, probably catching a fish to take home. Herby drifted around her once or twice. Then he pulled a little farther into the back eddy and things quieted down. The rip stabilized for a few minutes and we all paid attention to our lines in the water. When the inevitable finally happened, it actually took us by surprise. It happened that fast.

A sudden surge and the whirlpools changed their location again. All of the guides instinctively motored away from them to a safe distance—all of us except for Herbert. A whirlpool saw its opportunity and opened its foam-flecked mouth. Herbert and his boat dropped away from us.

Even though I only watched, the sensation of falling hit me in the pit of my stomach. Herbert, however, was still smiling at us as he slipped below our line of sight. His boat began to rotate as the hole opened to make room for him. The whirlpool widened out and we all looked down into it. Herbert continued to smile cheerfully back up at us from at least ten feet below.

Someone had to go down into this thing to get Herby out before his boat flipped over and dumped him into the raging tide. Every guide watching was faced with the same dilemma, though—we all had two customers in the boat with us. We would be putting their lives at risk to save him. We all paused.

That's when Gilly grabbed her knife and cut her line. Without hesitation, she gunned her boat forward. She caught the lip of the whirlpool and let it spin her inside. Her boat came alongside Herbert's. The weight of the extra boat opened the hole wider, giving them room to sit side by side, although pointed in opposite directions. The two boats circled each other in a death-defying spin.

"Jump in my boat!" Gilly yelled at him.

"It's all right," he yelled back. "This is a Nantucket whaler. It can't sink. I'll be fine."

"You need to get out of there now!"

"No, really, I'm not in any danger."

"What the hell is wrong with you?" Gilly reached out to grab Herbert. Her hand closed over the little leather knife case attached to the side of his belt. It was the perfect handle.

His boat began climbing the side of the whirlpool and tipped over on its side. She yanked on the knife case and he fell forward onto the floor of her boat. She had to let go of him to straight-arm his boat, to keep it from coming down onto her handrail and trapping her boat under it. It continued turning over and on top of her. She kept her arm on the bow of the overturning boat and pushed as hard as she could. She had to lift his boat away from hers, and she grunted out loud from the effort.

With her other hand, she gunned the motor and allowed the centrifugal force of the spinning water to give her enough speed to escape. She drove under Herbert's upturned boat. As she started to move past it, she gave another push, hard enough that it spun out into the tide.

Gilly gunned her engine again, Herbert now safe on the floor. She climbed the wall of the whirlpool, picking up speed. Her boat flew out of the white water, throwing spray and foam in all directions, right past me. The whole thing had happened so quickly, my guests hadn't finished reeling up. Her motor caught the lines that trailed out behind us. She came to a stop in the small bay just inside the point where the whirlpools formed.

I needed to untangle my lines from her motor. I also wanted to see how Gilly was, so I followed her into the bay.

"Are you okay?" I asked her. She was sitting with her head down between her knees, gasping for air, as I pulled alongside.

"I'm fine." Her face was still red from exertion. "I think—I think I'll just sit here for a minute and get my breath back, if that's all right. Uh, you guys, you guys just talk among yourselves." Gilly was having trouble talking. She put her head back down and held on to it with both hands. Of course, my guests immediately began telling her how incredible that was and that it was the most amazing thing they had ever seen.

I looked down at Herbert, who was now sitting up in the bottom of her boat.

"And you, Mr. Crane, how are you doing?" I asked him. Herbert stared wildly around him, like he was trying to make sense of what had just happened. He wobbled up onto his feet and sat down heavily in a guest chair.

"That was a brand new Nantucket whaler." He seemed incredulous. The latest thing in marine technology and it still wasn't enough to turn things in his favour. "They're not supposed to sink like that."

"Oh, it didn't sink," I said, and pointed toward the middle of the channel. The boat was already more than a mile farther down the tide. Its bow and the propeller of the big motor were the only things visible. A couple of guide boats were already there, circling the upside-down hull, making sure no one had fallen into the water.

"They won't sink, that's for certain, not the way they're made." I added, "They will flip though. So, have you met Gilly? You know, she probably saved your life today."

Herbert was still muttering about what the boat was supposed to do.

"What was that?" he asked me. "Why, yes, yes, I do. I mean, I am, I'm very thankful. I'm sorry she had to put herself in such danger."

He looked at his hands. The full realization of what had just happened was still settling in. His hands began to tremble. I turned to Gilly, who had gotten her breath back, though her hands were still shaking as well. She roused herself and ran her hand along the gunnel next to her chair. This was where the two boats came the closest, but it didn't look like there had been any contact. Herbert saw what she was doing and seemed to return to reality a little. He apologized to her again.

"I hope there is no damage," he said.

"There doesn't appear to be. Looks like the boats managed to miss each other." Gilly's efforts had kept the boats from colliding. She began to relax as well.

"Well, I'm certainly glad about that," said Herbert, already talking as if it had happened to someone else. "If you find anything, let me know. Perhaps I can help get it fixed. Anyway, you guys won't have to worry about me getting in the way again for at least a couple of weeks. We're getting ready for the maiden voyage of our company's newest ship. It's all very exciting. We'll have to have you both on board for dinner one night."

Sadly, it really was that kind of a summer. As things turned out, Gilly and I were never able to take Herbert up on his offer.

twenty  # EVEN A BURNING BOAT IS BETTER THAN NO BOAT AT ALL

WATCHING GILLY AND the adventures she was having in her first season brought back memories. No matter how you try to prepare, you will always encounter something you never expected. My first season of guiding at Stuart Island was the summer of 1978. I somehow managed to convince Mr. Carrington to trust me with one of his boats. Of course, he didn't give me the best one in the fleet. With two heavy customers and me, the boat struggled to get any speed at all. I arrived at the fishing holes after everyone else at not much more than trolling speed. It was so slow I spent most of my time at the mouth of Big Bay, fishing in the Second Hole on the flood, and on the other side of the bay at the Over Falls on the ebb. It turned out to be good practice and I soon learned the best way to catch fish there.

Sometimes I was bold enough to join all the old-timers and line up at the First Hole. You really had to pay attention. Here the tidal water rushed out of Big Bay past the point, and the big whirlpools began to set up. They were only three or four feet across to start, but you could see down them ten or fifteen feet, all the way to the rocks on the bottom. Once past the point they gradually flattened out, and by the time they passed the Second Hole, they could be fifty or sixty feet across.

A back eddy formed just behind the point, where the water was relatively quiet, and ran back toward the whirlpools. The guides took up positions along the edge of it and pointed away from the fast water. They had to use their engines, carefully giving them just enough gas to keep their boats in the right spot. They didn't want to drift too far into the fast water or get pushed away from the point.

The guides who fished there successfully had been doing it for years. Often fathers and sons fished next to each other, and fishing alongside them was a great way to learn. They used big cut-plug herring for bait. The head of the herring was severed with a very sharp knife at an angle. If the angle was cut properly the herring would do a very slow roll as it moved in the tide. If you got the hook baited with herring just right, and if you could hold position just right, you were guaranteed to catch a big fish.

If you were bold enough to fish there, you had to get in quietly and fish right beside people. You could not tangle their lines. It was quite useful to know how to change bait with one hand while you steered the boat with the other. Most importantly, when you did hook a big one, you had to be able to play it out into the rapids. You had to get past all the massive whirlpools, fast-moving ones being born right in front of you.

I managed to survive the big spring tides and was actually catching a few fish. In those days, it was hard not to. The summer was well underway and I was beginning to feel pretty confident, cocky even. Mr. Carrington was pleased. He wasn't pleased enough to give me a new boat, but he did replace the old outboard with a brand new twenty-horse.

Now I could go places. I could run up to the Log Dump at the end of the flood tide when the fish began to bite there. Mainly, the new engine gave me a feeling of safety when playing a fish into the rapids. I knew I could avoid the whirlpools. I had the power I needed to get out of the First or Second Hole. I began to look forward to the experience.

I even found I had more patience with the guests. Mere survival was no longer my main focus. I could engage in a conversation. If they were so inclined, we could share stories. I sat at the stern of Mr. Carrington's boat with new and bound-less confidence.

One afternoon in the Second Hole, the time had come for me to take my guests in for supper. I reached back to the new motor. With casual assurance, I grabbed the starting cord and pulled. Instead of the sound of a brand new motor starting, there was a loud pop! The front of the engine cover flew open. My arm disappeared in a tongue of flame that rose three or four feet into the air.

Yells of astonishment carried over the water from people in the boats around me. Some guides offered advice. The best suggestion was to undo the fuel line from the engine. I could not reach the side of the engine where the fuel line connected because of the heat and the flames. One of the guides saw the problem. He came up behind my boat, reached out, and unhooked the fuel line from the engine that sat outside the boat. Meanwhile, I unhooked the line at the tank inside, and then grabbed a towel. I soaked it in my bait tank, squeezed the water out, and threw it over the engine cowling to smother the flames. It snuffed out the fire as quickly as it had started.

I looked down at the smoking mess. The hair on my arm was singed off, but I had avoided any serious injury. I had not burst into flames myself. I took a deep breath.

Then I remembered the two other people in the boat with me, my guests. I turned toward the bow. They were both up on the boat's small foredeck with their knees pulled up, as if they were trying get away from a mouse. Their eyes were huge. They were ready to jump into the water.

"No, no, no," I offered helpfully. My brain was having trouble keeping up. I realized they might need something more persuasive.

"You see those whirlpools going past?" I pointed to a couple of sixty-footers. "If you got caught in one of those, we'd never see you again."

Perhaps this sounded too terrifying. I wanted to calm them down, after all. So, with as much reassurance as I could muster, I pointed to the still-smoking engine and I added, "Even a burning boat is better than no boat at all!"

twenty-one **WHEN TROUTBREATH WAS A ROOKIE**

YEARS AGO, WHEN Troutbreath was in his mid-teens, he had a summer job at a boat rental near Vancouver. He enjoyed spending the day down in the dock house, watching the world go by. He had to keep the boats bailed out, gassed up, and ready to go, and he had to prepare the herring to be used as bait. Each herring was basically filleted, cut into two equal strips off the side. Each one could be strung onto a hook in such a way that it moved like a live fish. He got so good at it that he could split the tail in two, leaving a tail on each fillet, which improved its performance in the water.

He also had to keep the rods and reels in good working order. Some customers weren't very careful winding in the line, so when the docks were quiet, Troutbreath would strip and rewind the reels. First he attached the hooks to a board on the dock house. Then he walked down the dock, letting the line peel out from the reel. When the line began to unwind smoothly, it had reached the undisturbed wraps. He would reel it all back in, making sure it was evenly wound. This was usually the last chore of the day, and once all the rods were well organized, he could spend the rest of the afternoon lying on a pile of life jackets. He looked forward to this time of day the most.

The owners of the boat rental trusted Troutbreath to look after things in the afternoon, but few people were interested in renting a boat at that time of day. Most of the serious fishermen went out early and were back before lunch. He could finish his chores at leisure, and then enjoy his lunch and some quiet time.

One particular day Troutbreath was already comfortable on the life jackets when the docks started to bob up and down more than usual. He resisted getting up. It was probably just the wake of a boat that was bigger than average, but something moved him to find out. He saw nothing on the water. He leaned out the dock house window to look back up the dock.

The largest human being Troutbreath had ever seen was walking in his direction. The guy was immense. With each step, the docks swayed in tandem, and each dock was almost underwater when he reached the end of one. Then it sprang back up as he stepped off onto the next. The closer he came, the more the dock house bobbed.

The man was wearing blue denim overalls and a cowboy hat. On his shoulder he carried a heavy metal cooler effortlessly, probably full of his favourite beverages. Beside him walked a normal-sized woman who looked tiny in comparison.

When Troutbreath noticed a chain around the man's neck with a horseshoe pendant, he realized he recognized the man from the newspapers and television. Only one person fit this description: Haystack Calhoun, the famous wrestler, who weighed in at 625 pounds, or so they said. His signature move was to simply land on his opponent, preferably from the top rope. That usually ended the fight.

Haystack approached the window of the dock house and explained that he wanted to rent a boat for a couple of hours, so he and his wife could enjoy a late lunch on the water. The window spanned the width of the dock house wall, and could accommodate two or three customers at a time. There was no glass, simply a piece of plywood hinged at the top, which Troutbreath swung up to a hook when he was there. The counter was just deep enough for the customers to write on as they signed out the boats and tackle.

Haystack filled the entire width of the window, with his wife peeking around his elbow at the very corner. Troutbreath knew he had a serious problem. A smile formed on his face and froze there.

"Ah," he exclaimed, just to buy himself some time.

The problem had to do with the weight of the man and the capacity of the boats. The boats available for rent were wooden with a clinker-built hull, each with a Briggs & Stratton single-cylinder gasoline engine. Most were fourteen-footers, and the biggest were seventeen feet, with a small cabin to protect the occupants from the wind. The maximum legal capacity of the largest seventeen-foot boat was 700 pounds. Haystack Calhoun's wife was probably about 140 pounds. Combine that with Haystack's weight, plus all the gear for lunch on the water, and Troutbreath legally couldn't rent him anything. Troutbreath knew the owners would stick by the regulations. He would have to find a way to break it to Haystack.

"Ah," Troutbreath said again.

The idea was a little daunting. Haystack filled the window like the trunk of a first-growth cedar tree, blocking all light. Troutbreath had seen him wrestling a couple of times on TV. He was convinced that Haystack was capable of popping Troutbreath's head like a grape, even by accident. Standing in the dock house didn't give Troutbreath a feeling of safety. Haystack could reach through the window and pick him up the way a regular person might reach into a cage and pick up a hamster.

He wasn't about to tell the guy he was too big to fit into one of the boats. Plus he actually wanted them to have a wonderful afternoon on the water; making that happen was something Troutbreath liked to do for people. He had to think quickly. Then it occurred to him that a man who was on television on such a regular basis would have certain expectations.

Troutbreath loved the finely crafted wooden boats he rented and was proud to send customers out in them. Just this one time he was going to have to undersell them, though it hurt to do it. He ventured out of the dock house and walked over to the wooden boats lined up along the float. He pointed a little disdainfully at them and tried to look embarrassed. He watched Haystack's expression change as he realized these were his choices.

"We just have these old wooden boats—you know, most of our guests just want to go fishing," said Troutbreath, trying to imply that Haystack wasn't "most" guests. "You and your wife might not find our boats as comfortable as you might like. Just over there, on the other side of the bay, our competitors have a couple of brand new, much larger fiberglass boats, with a proper cabin, and new outboard motors that are much bigger and more powerful than anything we have. I think you'd find them much more suited to the afternoon you have planned. Why don't I phone them from here to see if they have one available?"

Troutbreath picked up the phone. Once the owner of the competition learned who wanted to go out on the water for the afternoon, he took it upon himself to drive one of his boats over to Troutbreath's side of the bay to pick up Haystack and his wife. Once Haystack saw the modern cabin cruiser coming to pick him up, he looked greatly relieved. After Troutbreath helped Haystack and his wife aboard, the big man stopped and shook his hand.

A few days later, a letter arrived in the mail at the boat rental. It was addressed to Troutbreath, and inside was a lovely thank-you card, probably picked out by the wife. Along with the card were four front-row tickets to Haystack Calhoun's next wrestling match.

Troutbreath wasn't much of a wrestling fan, but he knew people who were. When he found out how much these people were willing to pay for the tickets, well, it was like a door had opened. Hanging out on a gas dock came with certain privileges and opportunities, and he was suddenly more inclined to spend time there.

The more Troutbreath did it, the more it became a career. One opportunity that came along was to take up residence at the Carrington's gas dock, and he he couldn't turn that down. Not only did his wages increase, though; his responsibilities did too.

He was getting so busy at Carrington's that he became nostalgic for the early days of the boat rental. He missed those afternoons dozing on a pile of life jackets to the sound of the clinker-built wooden boats rising and falling rhythmically on the moving water. The pace of the fishermen he dealt with then was slower, more enjoyable, unlike the frenzy that fishing had turned into at the Big Bay gas dock. Making people happy on the water, both guides and customers alike, was becoming too much like work.

twenty-two   **THE HOUSE MEETING**

DEALING WITH ANOTHER engine fire would have been preferable to the conversation I had promised Mr. Breland I would have. I finally arranged to have a chat with Vop and Carol one evening when we were all home

Vop and I sat tying leaders, and Carol lay on the couch, reading an Alfred Hitchcock mystery.

"So, you remember I was out with Doug Breland on the derby day, just the two of us?"

"This isn't going to be another one of your 'How I Won the Stuart Island Community Salmon Derby' stories, is it, Dave?" Vop was already getting a little tired of hearing about it. "Tell me that's not why you called a house meeting."

"I wish! But no, Breland actually wanted me to pass along some news. I'm afraid it's news that you need to hear. Doug told me his in-laws are selling the house on Cortes."

Vop looked at me blankly, a fishing line between his teeth.

"You know, your house. The one you've been staying in for how long now?"

You could almost hear the squeak of the wheels turning. He took the line out of his mouth.

"They're selling the place?" The idea that such a thing could ever happen obviously had never entered his mind. "No way.

— 87 —

Why would they ever do that? It's like nowhere else on the coast. Why would they give that up?"

"Well, maybe because it's overrun by island people with no clothes on? Mr. Breland did say they weren't having as much fun there as they used to."

"Oh man, it's like a bad dream. Do you really think they are going to do it?"

"Their son says so. I kind of take his word for it."

Carol closed her book, keeping her finger on the page, and looked up at us.

"How much are they going to sell it for?"

"I didn't ask," I said. "I mean, we all know how nice the place is. Your own white sand beach on the north end of Cortes? It must be worth thousands."

"People like us can never afford it, that's for sure," added Vop. "Not even if we cashed in all our BCRIC shares together." The BCRIC shares were becoming a sore point for him. His dad had most of Vop's university fund tied up in these shares. A couple of Vop's guests had been talking about them and it wasn't good.

"Ask him the price when you guys go fishing next," suggested Carol.

"Why? Why bother, it's too painful to even think about."

"I have a birthday coming up, and a girl can always dream, can't she?" Carol smiled enigmatically, an expression we were familiar with but were never quite sure what it meant.

twenty-three | # THE TROUBLE WITH CELEBRITIES

VOP MAY HAVE been distracted that day. It was hard to blame him, really. The idea of having to move from such a spectacular house to something totally unknown wasn't the easiest thing to reconcile.

He had an afternoon session of fishing booked with Morris Goldfarb. Morris had recently hosted another one of his benefits in Seattle for a hospital. The word was now out that some well-known celebrities were coming up to go fishing as a reward for their time and commitment to that worthy cause.

Vop reached the docks at Dent Island a little early. Since Gilly had begun fishing in the area, Vop found himself spending more time cleaning his boat than ever before. It wasn't a bad idea, having his boat cleaned up and looking organized, in case these people were as important as the rumours had it. A light rain was falling and Vop set about wiping down the guest seats.

Morris's yacht was quiet. Vop suspected everyone was enjoying lunch. No one was in much of a hurry to get out into the weather. As far as Vop was concerned, they could take their time. He had so much on his mind, the cleaning up and wiping down of his boat was the kind of mindless activity he needed right then.

He was standing in his boat, his back to the yacht, when he heard a heavy thump on the dock boards followed by the sound of someone running toward Vop's boat with a lot of momentum. He turned quickly and put his hands up. Before Vop could yell, the person leapt off the dock into Vop's boat.

The floor of Vop's boat was treated with crushed walnut husks to give it a sure footing, even in a gentle rain. However, the hard soles of the man's leather street shoes found no traction there. His feet went out from under him and he flew up into the air. He landed on his back on the floor of Vop's boat with a shocked look on his face.

Vop immediately recognized that face. One of Hollywood's most beloved leading men lay flat on his back in the bottom of Vop's guide boat. As far as Vop could see, the man's arms and legs were completely still, though he was able to move his head.

The enormity of what had just happened overwhelmed Vop. His brain, which was always so helpful in these kinds of situations, imagined himself a week into the future. Vop was standing in the checkout line at the grocery store, facing a rack of tabloid newspapers. Each presented a full-page photo of the actor, emblazoned with his name and the headline, "Rendered Quadriplegic in Boating Mishap!" In an inset in the bottom corner was Vop's photo and the caption, "Charged with negligence in movie star's fall!"

As Vop read the tabloid's front page, the people in the line with him looked at the picture in the corner and then at him. People began to edge away from him, whispering. Someone pointed at him. One woman reached out and swept her children behind her. One of the children peered around at Vop and started to cry.

None of this was very useful right now, and Vop forced himself into action. He knelt down beside the man, reached out toward him, and asked him if he was all right. Much to Vop's relief, the man took his hand and tried to get up.

"I guess you were trying to tell me not to jump into the boat, weren't you?"

"It's generally not recommended, sir," replied Vop.

Fortunately, the man was completely unscathed, not even a bruise or a scrape to show for his tumble.

"I guess that was quite the entrance, wasn't it?" said Vop's new celebrity friend, making light of the situation.

Vop helped him up into one of the freshly wiped customer chairs. Once he was safe and settled, they shared a bit of a laugh.

twenty-four **MR. ROSENVAND**

THE STUART ISLAND area was attracting a great deal of attention. Across from Big Bay on Sonora Island, a whole new resort was growing out of the side of a hill. I hadn't worked for them but I knew the guide who organized things on the water. One day he asked me if I was available for an afternoon with a new client. My friend heard I had a way with the older, more eccentric gentlemen. It was a niche that helped fill in my days.

When I reached the new resort, the dock was empty except for a young woman who sat watching the tide flow past.

"Are you here for Mr. Rosenvand?" she asked. "He's still up there getting ready. I'm sure he'll be down soon."

We waited quietly until the silence became awkward. Finally, she told me her name was Rachel and that she was a hairdresser who worked in a salon just a few doors away from Mr. Rosenvand's office. She washed and trimmed his hair at least twice a week. He was always trying to give her things, and not just small presents, either.

"He offered to buy me a car, a Cadillac, which I told him not to. He wanted to buy me a mink coat, but you know, it's a little old-fashioned these days. He finally asked me if I wanted to go salmon fishing up in British Columbia. He kind of wore me down, and I just said, why not? I mean, how often do you get a chance to do that? I know what people think—that I must be using him or that I'm a prostitute or something, but it's not like that. I really am just a hairdresser. He treats me like I'm his daughter."

"Hey, I hear stranger stories. I believe you," I reassured her.

Mr. Rosenvand finally made it down to the dock after I had been talking to his hairdresser for almost an hour.

"Are we going to fish here?" he asked standing on the dock and looking down into my boat. It took me a moment to understand what he meant.

"Ah, no, I thought we could go over there," I said, pointing to the Second Hole, just across the channel and no more than a couple of minutes away.

"Oh yes, I see. Are we going there now?'

"Let me help you into the boat and then we can go."

Rachel was watching all this with a great deal of knowing amusement. She hopped in and sat down, showing Mr. Rosenvand how it was done. He followed awkwardly. In a matter of a few minutes we were set up and fishing in the Second Hole.

What happened next needs a little perspective. To be clear, it rains at Stuart Island. Perhaps the best illustration of how much is the time I had a Scottish guy out. This was some years earlier, before things began getting fancy and the resorts began stocking rain gear and survival suits for various-sized guests. Back then, if you wanted to go fishing, you had to arrive at the island equipped for the weather. The Scottish guy was a last-minute addition to a business group. He really had no idea where he was going or what to expect.

That particular weekend, it was raining and raining hard. The lodge took pity on him and did the best they could to keep him a little dryer by giving him some green garbage bags. One was fashioned around his waist like a kilt, another had three holes cut out for his arms and head, and another one was tucked under a baseball hat and hung down his back. He looked a little like a green Lawrence of Arabia. It was raining so much that water poured down over the brim of his baseball hat. It was as if he was peering out from behind a beaded curtain.

"Aye," he said in his thick accent. "It really rains here, doesn't it? It's not exactly what you call your Scotch mist then, is it?"

This day was overcast, but certainly not raining. However, as Mr. Rosenvand sat in his chair, dutifully holding his fishing rod for me, I heard a "tsk" and turned to see him fiddling with his Fortrel pants. A fat little drop of water had landed squarely on a razor-sharp crease. Mr. Rosenvand tugged at the crease, but it now refused to stay up properly.

"Say," Mr. Rosenvand said, when he realized the extent of the soaking he had received. "Do you think it's going to keep on raining like this?" He indicated the wreckage the raindrop had made of his pants.

I didn't quite know what to say. I thought about what the man from Scotland had endured. There was no right answer to Mr. Rosenvand's question.

"I think we should go back to the resort now," he said before I could reply. "I want to get out of these wet clothes."

He was quite insistent. There was nothing else to do but what the customer requested. When we got back to the dock a few minutes later, another man stood on the dock idly watching the movement of the current. Mr. Rosenvand obviously knew him and greeted him by name.

"I'm calling it a day," said Mr. Rosenvand. "But if you don't mind the weather, Arland, why don't you and Rachel go back out with Dave?"

I ran them over to the Second Hole. The tide was still running and there was a good chance of picking up a spring salmon. The way Arland handled a rod and reel, it was quite apparent he had some skills. Before long we had a nice fifteen-pound spring salmon in the boat. Rachel sat up on the opposite gunnel as we played the fish through the rapids to help balance the boat. She was enjoying her time on the water.

With a fish in the boat, conversation flowed easily between us. Arland inspected my reels.

"That's a great reel, the Ambassadeur 7000. It's the saltwater model, isn't it? We use these fishing tarpon off the Florida Keys," he said, explaining where he had learned to fish. "Those tarpon put up a good fight too."

Arland Jones turned out to be the chief financial officer for Mr. Rosenvand's company. They had been working together for more than thirty years.

"How did you guys ever end up working together for so long? You and Mr. Rosenvand." I had noticed that, even after thirty years, Arland still called him Mr. Rosenvand. "You seem like such different people."

"Well, yes, you're right. Mr. Rosenvand isn't exactly what you'd call a glad-hander, if you know what I mean by that."

"I've met a few of them up here over the years."

"Mr. Rosenvand isn't much for golf, for example, and he has even less patience for it than he has for fishing. But I grew up in Florida and the place is covered in golf courses. So the meetings and business dealings that take place out on the golf course? That's where I take over. I'll sit in on the board meetings most of the time. Quite often we won't even know where Mr. Rosenvand is. He tends to travel around the country on his own."

"Not that I want to be nosy, but he's not the usual kind of guy we get up here," I said. "He's maybe a little eccentric."

"He is that. You wouldn't know it to look at him but he is probably one of the richest men in America. Most of your guests up here are wealthy, all right, but they have to answer to investors, boards of directors, and the Securities and Exchange Commission. They may have money on paper, but they can't always do with it as they please. Mr. Rosenvand lives in a totally different world."

"How is that?"

"He is what you call a sole proprietor."

"Meaning he owns his whole company? What kind of company is it, if you don't mind me asking?"

"Not at all. He and his wife started out in their kitchen. Shortly after the end of the Second World War, they started cooking up handmade potato chips and selling them at the local fair in the summer. It was a good product, and people bought as much as the two could make just in their kitchen. You know how it goes—they eventually bought a commercial kitchen that allowed them to make even more. Pretty soon they were selling at the state fair, and even with the new kitchen, they couldn't keep up with demand, just the two of them. Before long they had to hire some people to help out. Friends, mostly, people they knew from their hometown. They brought me in as a kind of consultant, and I helped them with the books and gave advice on developing their company in a fiscally sound manner. I helped them create a brand name. Back then it was just a state-wide thing, but by now you may have heard of it."

Arland mentioned the name of one of the most well-known potato chip brands, not only in North America but also the world.

"That's his company?" I said, slightly in awe despite myself.

"That's his. After his wife passed away some years back, it's his alone. It's quite a business, too. He owns all his production facilities outright and has almost no liabilities. He is selling one of the simplest products it's possible to make, basically adding value to potatoes. He makes half of every bag sold."

"And I'm guessing that's a lot of bags. Why don't you reel in and let me check your bait?"

"Me too?" asked Rachel.

"Yeah, let's start over on both sides."

"Let me give you an example of what I am dealing with on a daily basis," Arland continued, as he reeled his line in. "As I said, Mr. Rosenvand likes to travel around the US on a regular basis. He goes to our small-town sales meetings, where he's much more comfortable. He likes to make sure our product is as fresh as possible, so we have smaller production centres around the country. He'll just show up unannounced and visit our different facilities. He is used to running things."

I grabbed both lines and flicked off the herring into the water. Three seagulls fought over the discarded bait almost as soon as it hit the water.

"He doesn't like credit cards, though, or even having a bank card. He is what you might call 'old school.' He started out going into the bank and depositing his money himself. If he needed some, he would walk up to the teller and take some out. Of course, as the business grew, these transactions had to be streamlined. I mean, I couldn't let him walk around with a paper bag full of thousands of dollars. In order for him to access his money while he's travelling, I had to open all these different accounts in banks wherever he might choose to go. He, of course, insisted that they be interest-making savings accounts, and they are, and they do. Take a guess on how much money these accounts alone make him on a regular basis."

"I have no idea."

"How does $38,000 sound?"

"That's more than I make in a year." I heard Rachel make a small gasp.

I threw her newly baited line back into the water and she let it down, counting the passes of the level wind, the way I had shown her. Arland's line soon followed.

"That's how much he makes in a day," said Arland. He had enough fishing experience that he could talk and count at the same time. "And keep in mind, that's just the small accounts whose only purpose is to give him some walking-around money wherever he happens to be. Keeping it all straight and organized is enough to drive me a little crazy. He actually travels to these places on the Greyhound bus. I'll get a phone call from some out-of-the-way place and have to wire-transfer some funds to a Wells Fargo or open an account over the phone with some skeptical bank manager who has Mr. Rosenvand sitting in his office. It's the kind of behaviour that can cause problems."

"What kind of problems?"

A fish tugged on Arland's line and he began to let the line out. The tip of his rod bobbed but then the fish went away.

"Well, Mr. Rosenvand and his wife never had any children. Exactly what will happen after he passes is the heart of the issue. There are some relatives, cousins mostly, who would love to get their hands on this much wealth. They have already tried to prove he's not competent in a court of law, but the judge sided with us. You've noticed, I'm sure, that he is a bit eccentric as a person, but as a businessman he is quite a genius. He has never lost money on any of his decisions—in fact, quite the opposite, whatever he decides to do just adds to his bottom line. He'll come back from his bus trips with signed contracts and agreements from grocery chains that he has negotiated by himself, in his own way. Most of the contracts are sealed with a handshake and not much else. That's one of the reasons we're at Stuart Island. Have you met Mr. Tydesco yet? He grows potatoes on a massive scale, and we're here to have a meeting or two. Mr. Rosenvand uses so many potatoes that even if he can make a deal to save a few bucks on a ton, it adds a huge amount to his profit margin. Mr. Rosenvand is letting me handle the day-to-day meetings and attend the barbecues."

"Hey, I think I've got a fish," said Rachel, and all conversation stopped as we played her fish around the hole. It was a little twelve-pounder, the first salmon she had ever caught.

For the rest of the session in the Second Hole we covered a range of other topics, and eventually Arland asked me what I did in the winter. I pulled my portfolio out from under the bow and showed him and Rachel some of the things I had painted over the last winter. Rachel liked a couple of them in particular.

At the end of the afternoon we returned to the dock with a couple of salmon. While I was cleaning them, Arland came back down to the dock with an invitation to the resort that night, to use the hot tub and maybe have a drink or two on Mr. Rosenvand.

After supper at my house, I got back in my boat and headed to the resort. It was a beautiful night to be on the water. The northern lights were visible, very pale in comparison to what you see farther north, but still there making magic in the sky. The water put on a light show of its own as well, filled with tiny creatures that glowed in my wake like sparks.

Rachel was already in the hot tub when I arrived. I climbed in, and we talked as we waited. She told me Arland was in a meeting but Mr. Rosenvand would be joining us soon. She was as amazed as I was about the story we had heard. She knew he ran some kind of company but had no idea what it was. Mr. Rosenvand never bragged about things. She had seen him getting on the bus from time to time, and now she realized that when he said he would buy her a Cadillac, he actually could afford to do that.

He finally came down the walkway from the main lodge. He was wearing the same shirt and tie as earlier, but these were now paired with boxer shorts in some kind of expensive material and socks held up by garters. He carried his towel awkwardly, as if he had never carried a towel outside before.

He put the towel down on a bench and climbed into the hot tub, basically fully clothed, except for his shorts. I doubt he'd ever been in a hot tub before, either.

"Aren't you going to take your watch off?" said Rachel.

"Oh, it's waterproof. I'm sure it will be fine," he replied.

We sat there, not quite knowing what to say until Mr. Rosenvand brought up the subject of my paintings. Arland must have mentioned them. I had to get out of the tub, throw on a jacket, and retrieve the portfolio from my boat. We all ended up sitting in the hot tub going through the photos of my artwork in the portfolio together. Rachel pointed out the ones she liked as Mr. Rosenvand thumbed through them. The two of them in the water with their heads together made quite the picture, Mr. Rosenvand in his shirt, tie, and garters, Rachel in her bikini.

"What do these red dots mean?" he asked. I told him they were ones that had already been sold.

"That's fine then," said Mr. Rosenvand, "I will buy these two for Rachel and I want to have that one and this one on the other page." He knew Rachel couldn't very well turn him down, or she might hurt my feelings. He could buy her something to show his appreciation for her work after all, and to show appreciation for mine as well. We knew by then that he was more than able to afford it. In his own odd way Mr. Rosenvand turned out to be the life of the party.

On my way home that night the northern lights glowed in the sky and the bioluminescent plankton flashed in the water. All in all it had been a very productive afternoon. We boated a couple of nice fish. Mr. Rosenvand paid me very well for four paintings. And as I was walking down the dock to my boat for the trip home, Arland returned. He thanked me for all I had done and gave me a handshake. The hand that shook mine hid a small folded square of paper—a couple of carefully folded hundred dollar bills. I rode into Big Bay afterwards leaving a trail of stars in my wake.

 *twenty-five* **TIPPING**

TIPPING IS ONE of those things that can teach you about people. There are those who make a big show of it. They wave around a handful of hundred dollar bills and brag about how much they are giving out. Others, like Arland, approach quietly and offer a handshake that hides a carefully folded one hundred dollar bill. Sometimes it's not about the money at all. Tipping really is about conveying respect for the service received.

A couple of summers earlier I took out a couple of Japanese businessmen. At the time, I spent the winters in Victoria, where I was studying a Japanese martial art called aikido. It was taught in Japanese and, along with the names of moves such as *shomen-uchi* or *kote-gaeshi*, I was learning to count and to be polite in a form of Japanese that really belonged in the sixteenth century.

The two Japanese gentlemen I took fishing spoke very little English. The younger man showed a great deal of respect toward the older man, not unlike the deference I showed to the advanced black belts who taught me.

These two must have thought they were at the very edge of the known world. You can imagine their surprise when I addressed them in my sixteenth-century version of Japanese.

My ability to count came in handy when I showed them how to use the reels. I was quickly able to get them counting the passes of the level wind so they would know how deep to fish. The fact I was able to be so polite to the older gentleman was not lost on either of them.

Taking a break from the chaos of the back eddies, we motored to a spot where I caught a rockfish with them. I cut it up right there in the boat and served them sashimi. At the end of the session, they appeared to have enjoyed themselves in a way neither of them had expected.

As we parted company back on the docks, they stopped in front of me. The brand new floater coats that the resort had provided didn't fit very well. They were zipped up to the chin and the collars came up to the ears. The men's hands disappeared up the sleeves of the coats that stuck out to the side like pipes.

They knew there was another ritual to be played out, but they didn't know how to proceed. The older man nudged the younger one and said, "Uh, tip."

The younger man immediately understood, but he looked down at the outlandish coat he was wearing. He pulled up the coat sleeves and did his best to dig through his pants pockets. His hands came up empty and a worried look spread across his face. With no other option he started searching through the resort's floater coat. He was rewarded with a crumpled two-dollar bill. He quickly passed it to the older man, who very carefully opened it up and smoothed it out. He took his time to make sure it was as flat and presentable as he could make it, then folded it in half length-wise. He carefully tucked one edge between the thumb and forefinger of his left hand and held the other the same way in his right hand. He made sure the fold was pointed up before he extended the bill toward me with both hands.

Aikido is a very traditional martial art and we train with weapons, especially the traditional Japanese sword. The sword, being absolutely razor sharp, is handled in a very special way. I realized that the older man must have had the same training. He bowed toward me and offered up the bill in the same way you would pass a person the Japanese sword. Recognizing this, I also bowed and received the "sword" in the appropriate manner.

It was only two dollars. I have certainly received much bigger tips, but never have the bills been handed over so elegantly.

twenty-six **THE GHILLIEWETFOOT**

WHEN TROUTBREATH FIRST arrived at Big Bay, tipping was a source of much dissension among the guides. Over his first summer, he studied it thoroughly and passed along what he learned. Tipping became much more equitable, but Gilly had not yet been the beneficiary of this wisdom.

Shortly after leaving the dock one morning, she had to look at the customer in her boat with suspicion and disbelief. Gilly had been on the receiving end of so much teasing that she no longer knew when her guests were being serious anymore. He stood next to her, looking over the side.

"I'm sorry," she said. "I'm not quite sure I understand what you want to do here."

"Young lady," he repeated. "I'm not going to relieve myself over the side of the boat, especially with some cabin girl watching me. You need to take me to shore."

Gilly didn't know what the big deal was. With other clients so far this summer, taking a leak over the side of the boat hadn't been much of a problem. Sure, there was some awkwardness, and if she had to hear one more time about how deep the water was… Still, this guy was a paying customer.

"Okay, there's a small beach around the corner. I can drop you off there."

Only moments before, they'd arrived on the other side of the inlet. The lines hadn't hit the water yet and the big motor was still running. Now they quickly reached the shore, and she let the hull scrape up on loose rocks and gravel. The beach was shallow, but the boat still sat in a few feet of water.

"You're going to have to carry me," the man announced. "You can't expect me to walk through the water. It will ruin these shoes."

Gilly looked down at the shoes. They were a kind of loafer made out of shiny leather, with not one but two tassels. She doubted they had ever been off a sidewalk before this trip.

"Yeah, I can see the problem."

"What did you say?"

"I'm sorry, I said this should be no problem."

Gilly sized up the man. He was a little pudgy but not much bigger than she was, really. She could carry him all right, though the whole thing was just a little ridiculous. She hopped over the side. Her gumboots were high enough to keep her feet dry, but the rocks were very slippery. Without her weight, the boat floated a little higher and she pushed it farther up the beach.

"So, how do you do this?"

The man asked the question as if she did "this" on a regular basis. It occurred to her to ask some of the other guides later if they had ever had done it. The other guy in the boat was too busy smoking his cigar to be of much use. Gilly reluctantly turned around and invited her guest to try and climb onto her back. It was all very awkward.

He was heavier than he looked. Her boot slipped as she took her first step. She staggered and he scrabbled to hang on. A couple of more steps and she slipped with her other foot. This time she paused, waiting for the rush of cold water on her foot. Luckily, the water hadn't found the top of her boots. The man strained to hang on to her floater coat. He was making little squealing, pig-like noises in her ear. She waited a moment and regained her composure. Another couple of quick steps and she dropped him on dry land.

She waited as he disappeared into the bushes. It took him a few minutes to find somewhere far enough away and behind the trees. In fact, it took so long his fishing partner finally lost patience.

"Hey, Milton, you ugly sonofabitch," he yelled in the direction Milton disappeared. "Is this going to take all day? We still have some fish to catch."

Milton reappeared finally. Gilly directed him onto a large flat rock at the water's edge, a step up for the remount. However, she couldn't get a good grip on his legs this way, and he hung off her back with his ass hanging out awkwardly. She struggled back over the algae-covered rocks. This time, when her foot slipped, the hole it found was deeper. The seawater seeped over the top of her left gumboot and the chill water soon filled it.

She had to keep going. The man bounced around behind her, and with one gumboot full, it was much harder to navigate the slick rocks. She got to the bow of her boat and turned. The man put a hand behind him and managed to sit on the bow safely, swing his legs over, and return to the guest seat. Gilly hopped over the side, even though her left boot slowed her down. She sat down in the guide seat and thought about emptying her boot. She didn't want the man to see her do that—she was too proud. For the rest of the session water sloshed around one very wet foot.

Regardless of her discomfort, she still caught them a couple of nice fish, but the end of the session couldn't come fast enough. She stuck it out with a smile.

When Gilly dropped them off at the gas dock for lunch, Milton thrust some crumpled up bills into her hand. She counted up the tip after the men had left: a Canadian five and a two, a couple of American ones, and a Seattle Transit bus token.

"Not as much as you were hoping for?" asked Troutbreath, who had watched as she straightened out the small wad of bills.

"Oh, it's just so frustrating. I had to carry the pudgy one onto the beach so he could take a leak. Look at this." Gilly slipped off her left gumboot and emptied it over the side of her boat. "Oh man, I've been waiting to do that for an hour. My foot is never going to be dry again!"

"This whole peeing ashore thing happens from time to time," Troutbreath said philosophically. "Lucky Petersen is the only one I know who has never had to do what you did. Tell you what, if you let me have the transit token for my collection, I think I can help you out—at least as far as the tips are concerned."

He sat down on the edge of the dock and swung his legs into Gilly's boat.

"When I first started working here, people were always bickering about tips. Some got more than others, but it didn't have much to do with catching fish or even how well the guides got along with customers. It actually was a bit baffling. Guides were getting mad at each other, and word came down from Mr. Carrington that it had better stop. So, following Wet Lenny's example in his attention to detail, I started taking notes."

He stepped into her boat. "Can I just sit in your guide seat for a second? Maybe you can sit in the customer chair."

Gilly watched with some amusement as Troutbreath sat down and pretended to be her. He looked around him. He sat back and crossed his legs. Then he sat straight up on the edge of the seat. Gilly realized she did the same thing, and that somehow he knew this. He reached back for the engine tiller arm and then into the bait tank.

"I got the guides to tell me how much they were making, fish caught, you know, all the important variables," Troutbreath explained as he moved around. "We run about twenty house guides, and about five or six always received the best tips. But I couldn't find anything they had in common. So then I started tracking the boats themselves. Sometimes the guides swap boats, and that's how I noticed that the money followed the boat."

He then switched places with Gilly and had her get back into the guide seat. Troutbreath slumped low into the customer chair and crossed and uncrossed his legs impatiently. Gilly recognized most of her customers in his pantomime. Then Troutbreath sat up and looked around.

"Yeah, I can see what the problem is. Hang in there a minute. I'll be right back."

Troutbreath disappeared into the dock shed. When he returned he carried a small square of three-quarter-inch marine plywood with four holes drilled in the corners.

"Your boat has a standard-sized seat mount with a four-bolt pattern. Take your seat off its mount and maybe get some longer bolts and put this spacer in. It will raise your seat just a little bit."

"That's going to make the difference?" Gilly was more than a little skeptical.

"Trust me. Money is funny stuff. You know how water always runs downhill? Well, money always runs uphill. The boats that got the best tips, the guide seat was always higher.

It didn't have to be by very much, but as soon as we changed things, the tips started to even out. I haven't seen a balled up handful of small bills like that since we installed these in all the Big Bay boats."

 *twenty-seven* # WHEN ALL HECK BROKE LOOSE

MR. CARRINGTON COULDN'T put it off any longer. He really wasn't looking forward to it, and it might cost him a great deal of future income, but he had to have a talk with Heck Tydesco. It was a quiet afternoon. All the guide boats were out fishing, but he knew that Heck had stayed behind. He joined Heck on the back deck of his yacht. He had to get it all out at once or else he would lose his nerve.

"Mr. Tydesco, my wife and I have been talking about your very generous offer to paint the resort. We don't want to seem ungrateful, but, you see, we kind of like it the way it is. We want the trees to look like, well, trees and the rocks to be, you know, rocks."

There, he'd said it. He was willing to accept what came next. Heck's eyes narrowed. There was a long pause. Then Heck laughed.

"Goddamn it, Carrington."

Mr. Carrington was afraid of what was to come next.

"You people want things the way they are. I respect that. If you don't want the place painted white, that ain't no never-mind. This is your own place; you can run it the way you want. Hell, I respect you for getting up on your hind legs and telling me to my face like a goddamned gentleman. I could use more people like you. So many goddamn bootlickers and yes-men surround me, it's good to get damn opinions that don't agree with me. Now can I get you a drink or something? We've got some dates to talk about. I've got a lot of people wanting to come up here and do some fishing."

Mr. Carrington wasn't quite sure if he was hearing right.

"Now then, that Dave guy. So, he's some kind of independent or something? What does that mean exactly?" Heck had something else on his mind.

"Dave? Well, unlike the resort guides, he has his own boat and motors, and he acts like a freelancer. He works for all the resorts whenever they need an extra guide."

"So, he don't have any guaranteed work, then he just has to take what comes along?"

"Well, Dave has a certain reputation. Some of our more demanding customers think well of him. He gets requested quite often."

"Requested?"

"People ask to go fishing with him specifically."

"So, if I want him to work for me, then all I have to do is ask for him?"

"Yes, that's right."

"Hell, he's another one who ain't afraid to tell me what he's thinking. I have a feeling I can keep him real busy for the rest of the summer."

twenty-eight THE GEOLOGY LESSON

I WAS BECOMING a popular guy, which always complicates life. Mr. Breland saw fit to send me out fishing with his wife and daughter. He was being very quiet about the fish we'd caught and about winning the derby, but then he did things like this. It was the first time I had ever been trusted with any of the wives and daughters together. Not only were they a very precious cargo that needed to be kept well away from any danger, but I would also need to find my manners. Calling them ugly sons of bitches even by accident was totally out of the question.

I pulled up to the swim step at the stern of the family yacht. The highly polished teak and stainless steel of the step sparkled in the sunlight that reflected off the bright white hull of the ship and the moving water. Mrs. Breland, standing at the stern, looked more like a movie star than the wife of some businessman. Crystals flashed on her baseball hat, and her eyes hid behind sunglasses with huge frames. Everything about her said expensive. I helped mother and daughter step safely into the boat and made sure they were comfortable.

I explained that the tide was flooding and we were going to be fishing in the Second Hole just outside the bay. As long as I stuck to the "I'm your friendly local guide" script, I felt safe.

We pulled into the back eddy at the Second Hole, away from other boats. I cut up a couple of herring and got the lines ready. We drifted to the top of the rip and I had them let out the bait. You fished the Second Hole by starting out at the top and letting the current push you along the inside of the fast water moving down the channel. Near the bottom end you turn your bow toward shore and ride the inside current, swirling in the opposite direction back to the top. We joined the other guides and drifted around the hole like rides in a giant carousel.

It was a busy day in the Second Hole. We brought two nice fish into the boat, with nothing testing my ability to carry on a conversation. Unfortunately, at that point, Mrs. Breland suggested we go somewhere away from all the boats. Not that I could blame her; the Second Hole was turning into chaos. However, the alternative was trolling over on the other side of Bute Inlet, where we would no doubt need to talk.

The run over there seemed to take much less time than usual. I fiddled needlessly to get the lines baited and in the water. Then I had to sit in my guide chair, in full view. The longer the silence, the more awkward it became. Mrs. Breland and her daughter sat in the guest chairs looking slightly bored. It would be good to say something, to talk about anything, but I didn't know how to begin.

We were trolling up the inlet where a very steep part of the cliff face dropped into the water. We followed the contour of the shoreline, and as we came around a small point of land we saw a cave above us, a long narrow entrance into the solid rock. A few small but tenacious trees made a home on the ledge above the cave. Mrs. Breland waved her hand in its direction.

"My goodness, look at that rock," she said, in her plumiest, most bell-toned mid-Atlantic accent. "Why, it looks just like a vagina!"

I had passed this rock formation many times. Perhaps because of my more limited experience with the subject, I had never looked at it in those terms. Of course, now that Mrs. Breland had made the connection for me, I was never going to see it as anything else.

It certainly broke the impasse. We talked about guiding and what it was like taking out people like her husband. It occurred to me that this was exactly why I was never left alone with the wives. We talked about what went on behind the scenes at a fishing lodge. Mrs. Breland talked about Wet Lenny, who no longer worked as a fishing guide, and what he was like as a son-in-law.

"Was he always that accident prone?" she enquired. "I mean, especially anything to do with water. It's quite astonishing, really. Whoever gave him that nickname was spot on."

Inevitably, they asked me what I did in the winter and so we talked about art. Mrs. Breland was very interested when she discovered I had been to art school and wanted to see my portfolio. She invited me to come to their boat the next day to meet one of her friends. This friend and her husband ran galleries both in Vancouver and Seattle.

As it turned out, talking with Mrs. Breland and her daughter was much more interesting than talking to most of the men.

twenty-nine **MY CAREER AS AN ARTIST**

THE NEXT DAY I made sure to catch the limit of salmon for my guests early in the day. By the time I returned home, cleaned up a little, and headed over to the Brelands' yacht, things were already well underway. It was an older, statelier wooden vessel, a remnant from a more classic age. Instead of a set of steps just thrown over the side, it had an actual gangplank that led to the elegant fantail stern. The guests were all dressed in a way that also reflected a more genteel time, the men in crisp whites and boat shoes, the women in gauzy, free-floating pastels. The crew, all in white, tended the built-in bar and a table with appetizers next to it.

Mrs. Breland appeared magically from out of the crowd and greeted me as I stepped onto the fantail. She was a skilled and consummate host. We made some pleasant small talk about the day's fishing and where the big fish were caught. She carefully steered me through the milling guests until she had me in range of the woman I was to meet.

"Claire, oh Claire, this is Dave," she called out. "This is the young man I was talking to you about. Both Doug and I are very impressed with the art portfolio he has shown us. I think you two should get to know one another."

And then Mrs. Breland was gone, enveloped by the crowd that opened and closed around her.

"Brenda has certainly told me all about you! Although if she likes your work that much, you'd think she'd actually buy some of it, instead of parading you about like a show pony," said Claire. I was beginning to like her already. Claire was an older, shorter woman in a pale blue crepe-silk dress. She was a bit stout, with an ample bosom that, reined in as it was, formed a kind of shelf under her chin. She was obviously used to speaking her mind and being listened to.

"So, you went to art school? And you keep a portfolio, photographs of your work? And you show it to guests, people that you take fishing that ask to have a look. Have I got it right so far? And do you sell very many?"

I told her I did.

"And how much do you sell them for?"

I told her how much I sold them for.

"So, you meet with all of the richest people, many of them art collectors. You get to talk with and sell them your art for more than I can get for you through my gallery. What do you need me for? Don't answer that. I know exactly what you need me for. I've been playing this game for a long time. Come, I must introduce you to my husband."

She turned and took a glass of wine from the server, then turned back to me. She put the glass to her lips, a bit off centre, and a large dollop of the deep red liquid fell straight down, landing on her right breast. The thirsty silk fabric gobbled it up and the red stain spread across her chest. She dabbed ineffectually at it with a napkin.

All I could think at this point was, don't look at her breast, whatever you do, don't look at her breast. I pretended nothing at all had happened. It was then that the crab puffs caught her eye. She put the napkin down and picked up one of the delicious-looking pieces of pastry. She took a delicate bite. Pink filling squeezed out the other end of the pastry and landed on her left breast. At this point she became quite frustrated with herself. She leaned over the table and swept off the debris with another napkin, but again the thirsty fabric sucked up every bit of moisture. She now had two growing stains on her bosom. I was staring at the top of her head so intensely I was starting to quiver.

"Oh dear," she said, "I'm making quite a mess. Let's introduce you, and then you two can talk while I go get cleaned up." It was a nice enough recovery. She towed me over to her husband, who sat in a tall-backed teak deck chair. I was happy to leave the awkwardness behind us.

"This is that young man Brenda was talking about," she said as we approached his chair. "We've been having a nice chat, although I'm afraid he must think I'm quite drunk."

With that she started to lean on the back of her husband's chair. She missed it entirely and fell hard onto the carefully polished teak deck behind him. It caused a flurry of activity. Of the two men standing beside her husband, one of them was a doctor, and he immediately began to help. Two more men identified themselves as doctors. All I really needed to do was get out of the way. Claire was comforted, her vital signs checked, and an inspection for damages made. Finally, they carefully helped her to her cabin below decks.

We never did return to our conversation. And I also never found out anything more about the plans for the house on Cortes.

thirty **THE YES-MEN**

I APPROACHED THE two guys standing on the pathway to the Big Bay restaurant carefully. Troutbreath had pointed me in their direction. Heck wanted them to get some time on the water. Normally my guests would be waiting for me on the dock, raring to go, ready to climb into the boat before I could even get the ropes tied.

These two were definitely the ones I was looking for. Both of them wore windbreakers embroidered with "Tydesco Chemical." They were hunched over one of those spray devices similar to the one Mr. Carrington used to spray the apple trees. A pump pressurized it and forced out whatever liquid was inside. As I came closer, I realized they were spraying some weeds along the edge of the path. They didn't see me approach.

"Excuse me," I said from a safe distance. "Are you guys Big Bob and Little Bob? You want to go out fishing this afternoon?"

The two were the same size and height, so why they had these names was a mystery.

"Hey, yeah, that's us. No need to stand back there, though," said the one who turned out to be Big Bob.

"I just, well… It looks like you guys are spraying some weeds with that thing. I don't want to get downwind and maybe inhale some of…"

Big Bob cut me off quickly. "Oh, you don't have to worry about that. This here is completely safe. It works on the plant hormones or some goddamn thing. T'ain't dangerous to people, just dangerous to plants. We're trying it out on some of these here dandelions."

I must have looked skeptical about his reassurances. He sprayed a small quantity of the substance into his hand.

"Here, looka here. It's completely safe," he said, then brought his hand up to his mouth and drank the liquid.

"Oh, no, no. You don't—you don't have to do that." I had to wonder if it tasted as bad as it smelled. "Please, I'll take your word for it. I mean, if you guys say it's safe, I believe you. You don't need to drink it. What is it, anyway?"

"It's biotechnical, is what it is. Hell, we don't even know. We don't make it ourselves, we're Promotions and Marketing. Say, you want a windbreaker?"

The other one, who must have been Little Bob, spoke next.

"It's a damn sight safer than the last stuff we were selling, ain't it, Big Bob?

"Um, which stuff was that?" I asked, almost not wanting to know.

"He don't know what stuff that was," said Little Bob.

"And he's gonna be takin' us out fishing?" Big Bob started talking with his buddy as if I wasn't there.

"He's gonna hate us, won't he, Little Bob? He's not even gonna want to take us fishing."

"Oh yeah, he's gonna hate us."

"Why would I hate you guys? We've only just met," I interrupted.

"We're with Tydesco Chemical. You might have heard of it—we used to make that insecticide that almost wiped out the eagles in the continental United States. We were real sorry about that, weren't we, Little Bob?"

"Real sorry," said Little Bob to back him up. "But looking around at the trees, seems like they is doing okay up here."

"Um, sure, I guess they are." Some things we just didn't discuss with the guests. "So are you guys finished here? The boat's all gassed. I'm ready to head out if you are."

"That's good. No, we're ready to go. We just wondered if you'd be okay taking us out in your boat, seeing as how we, you know, how we almost wiped out all the eagles."

"In the continental United States," said Little Bob, to clarify.

"And that stuff, it weren't like it was all that bad, it was just too successful. We ended up selling way too much of it. That's really what caused all the problems. We're not going to make that mistake again. Are we, Little Bob?"

"Not this time," said Little Bob.

thirty-one **WEIRDVOPISTAN**

IT WAS CAROL'S twenty-fifth birthday. Vop had gone all out and caught her a fish. There was a great deal of fuss and preparation in the kitchen of our cabin. The table where we usually tied leaders was covered with the remains of birthday card construction. Some of the bits and pieces left over were from the newspapers Stan the Steamer had coloured for us. The debris on the table spoke of a sense of panic in the frenzy of activity. If I remembered correctly, this event, Carol's birthday, had been overlooked last summer.

Later that night after the meal, Carol wasn't about to let Vop off the hook easily. There was a certain amount of teasing over the course of the evening. Then he gave her the birthday card.

"No, really, I love the card you made me," said Carol as she tried to remove some coloured pigment from her fingers with a napkin. "Even if it is a little messy."

"It's the thought that counts, right?"

"Absolutely! Um, Stanley didn't have anything contagious, did he?" said Carol as she inspected a particularly stubborn stain.

"We didn't get any warnings from the hospital."

Carol looked thoughtful. She had more on her mind than Vop's homemade birthday card.

"Do we know anything more about the house on Cortes, like the price and when they are putting it on the market?"

"Mr. Giblin here has been slow. He hasn't found the right time to talk to his new best friend, Doug, yet."

I suspected I was being mocked.

"Not that it's going to do us much good anyway, and nobody we know can afford it."

"What if I told you I was going to buy it," said Carol. There was a gleam in her eye that Vop missed completely. Something about it made me think she was being serious. Vop, however, not usually attuned to nuance anyway, was quite sure she was joking.

"What," he said, "you find another diamond necklace behind a seat cushion?"

"It wasn't a necklace, it was a tennis bracelet. Actually a very nice tennis bracelet—forty-two Asscher cut diamonds bezel-mounted in platinum. And I returned it to Mrs. Tydesco, the proper owner. You're right, it would have been a healthy down payment. But no, I don't need to rob the lost and found if I want to buy something."

"Okay, sure, you can afford the Cowichan sweater at the general store, but we're talking about a log cabin on the north end of Cortes. I don't know why you even brought it up. It's a pointless conversation." I was obviously catching up on something these two had been discussing previously.

"So, in that strange little place you live in, what do you call it? WeirdVopistan? No one has any money?"

"Not that kind of money."

"Especially girls, right?"

"I didn't say that."

"Uh-huh."

"Look, no one we know can come up with whatever it's going to cost, not just you and not just because you're a girl." Vop was sounding a little defensive, even to me.

"And you're sure about that?"

"Yeah, there's nothing any of us can do."

"Okay, if you say so. We don't have to talk about it anymore."

"I'd be okay with that."

thirty-two **A SPOT OF BOTHER**

I KNEW WHEN it was time for me to leave Vop and Carol alone with the silence between them. I took the opportunity to fill the tanks for the morning and headed over to the gas dock. I found Troutbreath out on the dock pacing back and forth with his arms folded in front of him. He was leading with his jaw, always a sign something was up.

"Hey, Dave," he said, "are you guiding this evening?"

When I told him I had the night off, he pointed to a motorized saltwater pump at the edge of the dock.

"A fishing boat has gone up on the rocks the other side of the Dents. They can't keep up with the water coming in and need this pump as soon as possible. I've been waiting for the first one of you guys with no guests."

"I guess I'm it. I have to gas up first."

"There's no time. Just grab one of the lodge tanks over there. Sounds like things are pretty bad."

Troutbreath helped me switch tanks and drop the pump into the bottom of my boat. I cast off quickly and as soon as I was clear of the docks I opened up the throttle. The boat jumped up on plane and I sped off into the growing twilight.

Heading out to the Dent Rapids, especially in the fading light, was not something I took lightly. They were scary enough in broad daylight. Plus it was a flood tide, and on the flood a whirlpool can set up almost the full width of the channel, over ninety feet across. Though it sits in one spot, it spits out smaller ones. By smaller, I mean fifty to sixty feet, about the size of the ones in the Yuculta or Arran Rapids around Stuart Island.

Lucky Petersen and I tried fishing the back eddies there once. We quickly decided the water was just too strong and unpredictable. The back eddies that did set up weren't stable. You could be safe away from the riptide one moment and then in the middle of a huge upwelling the next. We had a hard time just manoeuvring the boat to safe water, never mind doing it with lines in. Lucky pronounced it not worth the trouble.

I worked my way along the righthand shore as I left Big Bay. I could make out the rip line setting up off the point. I backed off on the throttle and picked my moment to jump the whirlpools. The boat bucked and shuddered and I could feel the kick to the water. The precious pump rocked around on the floor of my boat. By the time I reached the Dents, the rapids would be even stronger. I had to admit to a nicely developed sense of dread. It wasn't Troutbreath's fault. It was the way things were done. If I had been working this evening, whoever else was available would be out here, doing the same thing.

Once past Jimmy Judd Island, it's pretty much a straight run to where the fishing boat had gone aground. All you had to do was keep your hand on the tiller arm and the boat pointed in the right direction. Well, that and try not to think about what lay ahead. The problem is, on the water, there is nowhere to hide. I had to find something else to occupy my mind.

A couple of weeks before I left for the summer at Stuart Island, my aunt had given me a copy of the transcript of my father's logbook. He ran away to sea when he was about sixteen. After a few years on the fishing smacks that worked the North Sea, he joined the British merchant marine. He kept a log of all his travels, some entries not much more than longitude and latitude with a comment on the weather, from the various vessels he worked on. You could track his progress on a chart.

When the Second World War began, he saw no reason to stop the log entries, though writing this information down was completely illegal. As a result, he was probably one of the few ordinary seamen who could say exactly where he was during the war.

Over his years at sea, he had accumulated more than a dozen such books, each small enough to carry in his pocket. They then sat in a drawer in my parents' bedroom dresser for years. We all knew they existed, but none of us except one of his sisters could decipher the writing. She finally convinced him to let her transcribe them.

Some entries made you wish there was more. He downplayed most of his experiences; you might think that the entire Second World War was nothing more than a spot of bother, a phrase he used more than once in his log. In one entry, he describes being in a convoy heading to England from Halifax when the German battleship *Bismarck* came out hunting. All the convoy escorts left to help search for the *Bismarck*, leaving the convoy completely defenseless. At a top speed of about eight knots, the ships of the merchant marine were sitting ducks. The British navy sank the *Bismarck* before it reached my father's position.

He records another time when his ship was travelling up the African coast. The convoy was strung out in a single file. Suddenly, the ship in front of his blew up and sank. The convoy was being attacked by a submarine. The submarine then had to make a turn so it could bring the aft torpedo tubes to bear. The manoeuvre took a bit of time to complete, which probably saved my father's life, for a few minutes later the ship behind his blew up. At eight knots, evasion doesn't work very well. I had plenty of experience in not evading anything with my first guide boat. It could barely make eight knots, especially with two large guests on board.

Though there was a war on, people on both sides tried to do things according to certain traditions of behaviour long observed by mariners. The submarines stopped to pick up survivors of the torpedoed merchant ships, despite the danger involved with being on the surface and thus vulnerable to attack. The convoys also travelled with rescue boats that would stop and pick up survivors after a ship was sunk, but they were not considered hospital ships and could be attacked at any moment.

When I thought of the battleships and torpedoes from submarines that my father encountered, what was one whirlpool? At least that was what I tried to tell myself. The whirlpool at the Dents didn't care what I thought about it.

While the battleships and submarines of the German navy were certainly a threat, one entry in the log in particular suggests it may not have been the worst my father faced. On March 22, 1944, he was in port at Gibraltar, waiting for repairs to his ship:

> Still being repaired. All the women have been evacuated from Gib. [Gibraltar]. Did another Oerlikon firing course at towed sleeves. New weapon showed us—Pillbox—6 rockets on each side. "Quite safe," said old RNPO [the petty officer]. Volunteered to fire it. Top brass all turned up to

see demonstration on the edge of a steep cliff. So I sat in seat—old PO in behind. Pressed pedal and watched rockets exploding in sky. Clouds of smoke and found one rocket was still in rack and burning. PO on floor in ball. I suggested we throw it over edge of cliff before it blew up. Then the brass who had run away (they called it retreating to a safe distance) gave us hell for throwing it away as it should have been examined. However, they did not pursue it too far with me.

My father didn't talk much about his service. He admitted he was pleased his sister had preserved the contents of his log, but he didn't comment further. I learned some things about my father's legacy to me—such as my natural suspicion of the "top brass." And, gained somewhere along our time together, the ability to do what needs to be done, whatever the challenge.

Usually, if I run through the Dent Rapids, I am on my way to Frederick Arm or Estero Basin and I take the small narrow passage between Dent Island and the mainland, Canoe Pass. It's more like a creek than an ocean passage, but if you are careful, it's much safer. Then you follow the mainland side, avoiding the worst rapids. However, the fishing boat that was in trouble, which had to stay in the deeper main channel, was aground on the Sonora Island side, just north of Little Dent Island.

As I approached, I could sense the big water as much as hear it. It made the air electric, and my skin tingled. I navigated as close to the Sonora shore as I could. It was still light enough to see where the whirlpools were setting up. I just had to stay out of their reach. The rapids surged around me, trying to run me up on the rocks. The tiller arm kicked and tried to jump out of my hand. Hitting a rock was obviously a problem, but so was the bull kelp growing there. The big leaves that spread out over the surface can wrap around the leg of your engine and block the water intake. If that happens, the engine overheats, and it can seize up in a matter of minutes.

I turned into the surge and let it carry me away from the danger. The tide was running so hard by now that the water passed beneath me at great speed, while my boat sat in one spot, struggling to head in the opposite direction. I was going nowhere. I opened up the throttle and tacked into the current, turning from one side to the other to give myself a forward motion. I watched the rocks to check my progress. The surge died back a little, opening up some smooth water, and I ran along it before another surge hit.

I came around a small promontory, and there was the fishing boat, a classic white wooden salmon fishing troller. It sat up on the rocks like a broken swan, its system of long poles and pulleys all knocked askew by the impact of hitting shore. Over the rushing of the water came the sound of a bilge pump working flat out. A man waved at me from the stern.

"I have the bilge pump from Big Bay for you," I yelled, as I pulled up alongside.

"Man, am I ever glad to see you. The pump I've got can't keep up with the water coming in. I was afraid I'd lose her." His voice carried much fondness for his fishing boat.

"Let's see if we can prevent that."

Between the two of us, we heaved the pump in my boat into the stern of his. He snaked the intake hose into the fish hold and threw the overflow hose over the side. The motor started at first pull and a huge gush of water began spewing over the side, back to where it came from. With both pumps running, the battle evened out. The man looked very relieved to see the water in his boat receding.

"I can't begin to thank you enough," he said.

"I'm only the delivery guy. Really glad to help."

"Don't be too modest, I've seen how you guides run through the water around here. I couldn't do it. You still have to get back to Stuart, though, don't you?"

I nodded in agreement. I was also trying not to think about the return trip.

"Looks like things are okay for now. I can look after it from here. You'd better leave while there is still some light. Give them my thanks at Big Bay and tell them I'll get the pump back to them as soon as possible."

We shook hands and I took off into the darkness. I was glad to be running with the tide. It had backed off a little from my first trip through. The smooth water stayed in place and quickly took me into the calmer part of the channel.

As I passed Dent Island, I noticed the lights on in the main lodge. The guests there, smoking cigars, drinking, and bragging about their fish, would have no idea of the small drama taking place a short distance away.

Of course, Vop had no idea either. It was quite dark by the time I got back to our dock. I found Vop rummaging around in the stern of his boat.

"I thought you were just going over to the gas dock," he said. "What took you so long?"

"Oh, Troutbreath had a spot of bother and I wanted to help him out. Um... What are you doing down here in the middle of the night? You're not cleaning your boat, are you?"

"Well, you know, just tidying it up a little. What's this about a spot of bother?" I knew when Vop was trying to change the topic.

"Troutbreath just had me moving some rusty old pump for him. Say, you and Gilly are working that large party of fly-in clients tomorrow, aren't you?" Seeing him clean his boat, at that late hour, made me realize he wasn't really interested in my spot of bother. He had more than enough of his own spots to remove from his boat before morning. We both did.

"I have no idea what you're talking about," said Vop. He knew he'd been caught.

"I'm fishing with the same people. In fact, my boat could use a quick go over too. Are you finished with the long-handled scrub brush?"

We both stayed out there in the dark, cleaning away, until our boats were ready to fish next to Gilly's.

thirty-three **HOLE-IN-THE-WALL**

THE NEXT MORNING I was at the Big Bay dock picking up some herring and switching out the gas tank I had borrowed. I noticed Carol on the fantail of the Breland's boat. She and Brenda Breland had their heads together over a cup of coffee.

When I got back for lunch, they were gone. Both of them had caught the mail plane into town. There was obviously something going on. My impression turned out to be correct. Vop eventually filled me in on all the details, although he had to calm down first before he could find the words.

Before Carol flew off with Mrs. Breland that morning, she left a message for Vop. Carol knew it was Vop's turn to go shopping in Campbell River the next day, and her message told him to meet her first at the Swiss Chalet at the south end of town for lunch at eleven o'clock sharp, or else. The message also advised him to book off the next day, if possible, and to maybe get Gilly to cover for him.

"I feel like I've been summoned," said Vop when Trout-breath gave him the message.

"You have, my good man," said Troutbreath, "and the Swiss Chalet too. You'd better be wearing a clean shirt."

There was a certain amount of whining from Vop that night. Getting to town for an eleven o'clock lunch meant getting up earlier than usual. Vop was very protective of his sleep time. Still, he managed to get organized and left the house more or less on time.

Vop set off in his boat into a cold, blustery summer morning. The sky threatened rain, and he was dressed accordingly. He left the shelter of Stuart Island, heading south toward the Rendezvous Islands and Heriot Bay on Quadra Island. Out in the more open water, the wind slammed into him, sending a stinging cold spray into his face. He decided to take the more sheltered route through Hole-in-the-Wall.

Hole-in-the-Wall is a very narrow passage between Sonora and Maurelle Islands. In some places you could almost throw a stone from one side to the other, especially at the west end. On a big tide, when you had to watch for the rocks on either shore, it wasn't the easiest way to reach Heriot Bay. This day, though, the tides were small and the west-end passage would be safe enough.

As Vop entered Hole-in-the-Wall, the sun began to poke through the clouds. At the far end of the passage, the sun's rays picked out the telltale spray of a killer whale surfacing. More whales followed behind, their spray turning into rainbows in the sunlight. A family group was headed toward Vop, filling the channel. There was nothing to do but pull over into the kelp and wait for them to go past.

Vop shut off his motor and watched. They all surfaced together. Vop could hear their relaxed exhalations and then something more. His fish box, built into the side of his boat, acted like a sound box and amplified the song the whales were sharing. They called and answered each other, and Vop could make out the high pitch of younger calves.

One of the young ones broke away from the pod and swam over to Vop. He watched it swim under his boat and come up on the other side, between Vop and the shore. If it wanted to, even this smaller whale could have easily flipped Vop into the water with its tail. As its head broke the surface, it sprayed Vop with a fine mist, almost as if trying to get his attention. Vop looked over the side of his boat, down into the water, into the face of the most intelligent creature he had ever encountered, human or non-human.

The young whale looked back at him. Vop had the distinct impression it was smiling at him, as if, somehow, the whale had heard about him and all his antics. The whale regarded him with keen interest and cocked its head to one side. Vop, without thinking, reached his hand out and gently rested it on its snout. The whale flicked his head, not to knock his hand loose but to nudge it in a way that made Vop want to caress it. Vop petted the whale the way you might stroke a beloved dog. The whale lingered for a few moments. It nudged Vop's hand again until it had enough petting, then slipped effortlessly down into the water. The shadowy shape turned and headed back to the pod, which had almost reached the mouth of the Hole-in-the-Wall, the same way Vop had come in.

thirty-four  VOP GOES TO TOWN

VOP HAD SPENT more time with the whales than he should have, given the timetable he had been given. He had yet to reach Heriot Bay, where he would have to change, start the car—it wasn't used often, so starting it might take some effort—and hope to make the ferry to Campbell River on time.

At Heriot Bay, he tied up at the government dock. By now the sun was out. Vop stripped off his heavy rain gear and peeled back a couple of layers of clothing. He stowed it all under the bow of his boat and took off running for the parking lot. He was in sight of the car, then he stopped, turned around, and ran back to the boat. He remembered his car keys were still in his wool pants. He returned to the car with his keys but then remembered his wallet was still in the pocket of his rain jacket. By this time Vop was a little out of breath. Fortunately, the car started first try. Vop reached the ferry dock on the other side of Quadra just in time to see the ferry leaving.

He would have to wait for the ferry to drop off the cars and passengers at Campbell River, load, and then return. Perhaps it was all his recent exercise and shortness of breath but, as he looked out at Quathiaski Cove and the ferry disappearing around the corner, his eyes took on a faraway look. The thousand-mile stare, we called it. It was a thoughtful look, one that might suggest a deep struggle with the vagaries of life. Women found it attractive.

I had sad news for the women in Vop's life. I knew exactly what occupied Vop's mind. I knew because he had shared it with me once. I had seen the look and had called him back from the depths. I had to ask him where he went. Vop told me it was something that had been going on since he was a small child. It began during those Saturday mornings lying on the rug in his parents' living room, watching television—cartoons of course, or sometimes the *Captain Puget Show* out of Seattle. He couldn't really recall most of the shows he'd seen, but he knew one particular jingle. One of the show's sponsors knew their target audience, and knew how to get their message across. That simple little jingle had wormed its way far into Vop's brain and become permanent.

As he sat looking at nothing out the car window, it played over and over. It went like this:

Squirrel Peanut Butter is the best by far,
Creamy smooth to the bottom of the jar.
Get some soon 'cause you'll want more.
Get Squirrel Peanut Butter at your grocery store.

Vop had given up trying to stop it. He hoped that, given enough time, it would fade away on its own, but the stupid little tune always bided its time until it saw an opening. Vop didn't even like peanut butter.

The ferry finally returned and Vop was the first to load. When it reached the other side, Vop was in a panic to drive off. It seemed to take forever for the ship to dock and the car ramp to drop into place. He drove south to the restaurant, impatiently weaving in and out of the light traffic. He pulled into the first parking stall he found and raced out of the car to the front door.

When he got there, he saw a sign that stopped him cold. It read:

NO SHIRT

NO SHOES

NO SERVICE!

He had dealt with the implications of such a sign before. He had tried to whine and wheedle his way past the hostess at worse places than this, without success. Today it wasn't the shirt that was the problem. He was wearing a serious shirt. The shirt still had identification patches that certified it as an appropriate shirt for the uniform of none other than the Canadian postal system. Plenty of confirmation even for the pickiest hostess.

No, it was shoes that were the problem. He had left Stuart Island wearing his best black gumboots, which were now tucked neatly under the bow of his guide boat. Left behind because they were too hot to wear when the sun came out. He had driven to the Swiss Chalet in his bare feet.

Vop knew it was pointless to argue with the front desk people. He raced back to the car, hoping to find something to cover his offending lower extremities. There was nothing in the front or back seats. He popped open the trunk, which revealed layers of life. On top were the things he had brought along for the last camping trip he and Carol had taken before this guide season started. Beneath that were more layers, going right back to his time as a student. He dug down deep.

Way back in the far corner of the trunk, his hand found something, almost as if by instinct.

Carol looked up to see Vop advancing toward her table, where she sat with Mrs. Breland. Vop looked very pleased with himself.

"Hey, I'm sorry I'm late." It was now a quarter to twelve. "There were killer whales in Hole-in-the-Wall. I had to wait them out and missed the ferry and..."

"Are you two going out dancing later?" Mrs. Breland asked.

Vop stopped talking in mid-sentence and his face reddened.

"Those are quite the dancing shoes," she continued.

"Uh, hello, Mrs. Breland. I didn't expect to see you here."

"Oh, my dear, I wouldn't miss this for the world."

"Is that one of the liver sandals you're wearing?" asked Carol. Vop grinned at her sheepishly. It was indeed one of the sandals he had made from the especially tough liver served at the university cafeteria when he was going to school in the Kootenays.

"Well, um, they wouldn't let me in here without something on my feet."

Vop looked back furtively at the front of the restaurant. A rather skeptical hostess was still watching his progress.

"And you could only find one of them?" Carol continued. His right foot wore his homemade sandal. His left foot was carefully wrapped in tinfoil from the camping supplies. His foot looked like a baked potato.

"I'm such a lucky girl," said Carol to no one in particular.

"Is that one of the famous liver sandals? You know, when you told me that, Carol, I thought it was another one of those guide stories. Another story that sounds like fun but isn't really true. Yet there it is." Mrs. Breland sat back with a glass of white wine in her hand and admired Vop's footwear. She seemed to be enjoying herself.

"You know about the sandals?" asked Vop, a little incredulously.

"We do talk, you know," added Mrs. Breland. "What do you think goes on at the resort when all you men are out fishing?"

She had just confirmed all his worst fears.

"Anyway, like I said, I'm sorry I'm late ..."

"Oh, you're not late," Carol said.

"What do you mean? Your message said to be here by eleven sharp, but then there were these whales, and ..."

"How well do you think I know you? I told you eleven, but I told everyone else twelve."

"Everyone else? There are more people coming?"

"Yes," Carol answered succinctly. "And it looks like this is them now. Maybe you could, you know, sit down and hide your feet under the table or something."

The whole meeting unfolded before a rather bewildered Vop. He was introduced to a real estate agent who represented Mrs. Breland. Carol's lawyer he knew, and another real estate agent apparently represented Carol. The men wore expensive suits and shoes to match. They had all visited a barber's shop recently. Wordlessly, they joined the table that obviously had been reserved for just this number of people. There was a level of organization to all of this that Vop usually didn't experience.

Carol's lawyer opened up his briefcase and presented a cashier's cheque for the sum of $138,569 to Mrs. Breland's real estate agent. He opened up his briefcase and deposited a thick file of papers, marked with little clear-plastic page markers, onto the table. The markers opened at places for signatures, both Vop's and Carol's. The agent, who had obviously done this a few times before, expertly flipped to the right locations, murmuring, "Sign here and here. Initials here."

Vop simply did as he was told, still not quite comprehending all that was taking place. Carol quietly explained to him, in that voice she used. "This is just to confirm that it's a simple cash sale. No financing needed, so sign where the man says. The cheque covers the price of the land and all necessary fees and commissions. And this, this is the deed you'll need to sign in a couple of places. It means we both own an equal share in the property named below."

Vop had never seen a legal land title before. The document contained a list of numbers and a little map. It all looked like a math equation. He didn't recognize what it was right away until, somewhere near the bottom, he saw the words "Cortes Island." His brain slowly registered that somehow they were actually buying the Cortes cabin, and not only that, they were doing it with cash.

Later, Vop would remember the guys in suits leaving as efficiently as they had arrived. He knew he, Carol, and Mrs. Breland had stayed and enjoyed a lovely lunch, but he couldn't recall what he'd eaten. It was Swiss Chalet, so it must have involved chicken. He remembered Mrs. Breland making a point of telling him what a wonderful young woman Carol was. A woman of some means, at that.

He did some grocery shopping for our house that afternoon, but rather half-heartedly. He and Carol were going to stay in town as kind of a celebration. Carol's idea of celebrating these days was having a shower in a clean bathroom with endless hot water.

It didn't really sink in until Vop was in finally in bed that night at a motel. He laid on his back staring at the light patterns the city threw up onto the ceiling, trying to understand what Carol was saying.

"Okay, can you go over it all from the beginning just one more time? I mean, exactly how did you come up with a cheque for the full price of a prime piece of island real estate? How is that possible?"

"You remember the gravel pit and the little caretaker's cottage I lived in? The one you visited that particular evening when you tried to replace the Canadian Tire catalogues with toilet paper? It belonged to my grandfather. That cottage on a gravel pit was where he and my grandmother lived while he started his business.

"It was his first gravel pit, but he soon became the biggest supplier of sand and gravel in the West Kootenays. His gravel pits supplied the building of roads and railroad track beds. Most of the concrete that went into the bridges and buildings around there came from his operations. Then he used it to build himself some office buildings and maybe a hotel or two. My parents took over the business when he retired and built it up even more."

"But you were paying rent there and using old catalogues for toilet paper." Vop was having a hard time with all of it. He rubbed his forehead and drew his hand down the side of his face. He had created a spectacle of himself on many occasions, but he recalled that night as being particularly impressive.

"My grandfather was a simple guy. He wanted me to know the value of a dollar. My parents happened to agree with him, and when I turned thirteen, they sat me down and explained it all to me. As I was their only child, I would be inheriting everything they had. So, when I turned eighteen, I was going to be on my own, with no help from the family. They wanted me to go to school, but I had to pay for it all. They wanted me to be able to do things for myself."

Vop sat up to look at her. "So that's why a summer in the islands was such an attractive idea? It wasn't only my charming personality that drew you here?"

Carol ignored his charming personality and continued.

"Meanwhile, they set up a trust. When I turned twenty-five, I would get the first disbursement. At the age of thirty, I would come into the full estate. By that time, my parents would also be retired. The estate by then would consist mostly of shares and real estate holdings that provided a substantial income. My parents told me to develop some lifelong hobbies, because once I turned twenty-five, I wouldn't really need to work anymore if I didn't want to."

"What? They wanted you to have hobbies? That's why they sent you off into the world? So, what does that mean, cleaning up after fishing parties, making beds, and being a housemaid on boats is your idea of a hobby?"

"No, silly, it's called a job."

"That doesn't leave you with any hobbies though."

"That's where you're wrong, Mr. Great Big Fishing Guide. It's you. You're the hobby."

Carol reached out and held his chin in her hand affectionately. Her hand didn't linger for long.

"That's some growth on your chin there, Bucko. The shower is yours when I'm finished."

Vop reddened a little.

"But . . . you could have told me."

"Well, my grandfather didn't want me to talk about it. And he was right. People acted differently around him when he started to become successful. He wasn't naïve. He knew people would treat me like that if they knew I had money. He wanted me to experience life. And trust me, hanging out with you, that's exactly what I'm experiencing. And by the way, the next time you're staying at the gravel pit house, I'll show you where we keep the toilet paper—somewhere the mice don't steal it to make their nests."

thirty-five ## SUPPLY AND DEMAND

IT DIDN'T MATTER if a customer hired a first-year guide or someone as skilled and practised as Lucky Petersen, the cost of going out in a guide boat was always the same. Sure, it helped to know who to ask for, and some people had been coming so long, they reserved the guide they wanted, but the resorts all charged the same amount. It was perhaps the most democratic thing about the whole place. It drove Troutbreath just a little crazy. He didn't want to undercut the competition; he wasn't that kind of guy. But he knew for a fact that people would pay almost anything for a chance to go out with Lucky any day of the week. Why not maximize the earning potential?

This was becoming even more of a problem with Gilly. The word was out. The women had been coming back to the dock, day after day for most of the summer, with more fish than most of the men. The men were finally beginning to catch on. Going out fishing with the "cabin girl" had become something to brag about. Gilly was turning into a rare and desirable commodity. Unfortunately, unlike the herring swimming around in the reserve box, there was only one of her.

Her notoriety finally caught the attention of Heck Tydesco. It was only a matter of time before he wanted to be seen out fishing with "That Cabin Girl." Troutbreath turned him down at first; Gilly was already fully booked, after all. Heck simply offered her next clients a trip up to see the glacier in his helicopter and suddenly she was free that day.

Gilly was in the Near Side again, with Heck in the boat. It was just the two of them that morning. He had her all to himself and no doubt was looking forward to letting everyone know. The Near Side was still producing some great fishing and after the incident with Herbert Crane, no one but fishing guides went there. It was a big ebb tide that day, and as the velocity of the current began to build, people started leaving the hole with a fish on.

Then I saw Heck hook into something, and he and Gilly left the back eddy and quickly followed some monster into the main channel. His rod was bent over double and Gilly moved beside him to let the drag off a little. She expertly steered them through the whirlpools that formed, the rod bouncing and whipping this way and that as the salmon tried to shake out the hooks.

From where I sat, it looked like the fish wanted to sound, to get onto the bottom of the channel where it could sit and sulk. I knew this could be dangerous. The fish might snag and break the line on the rocks around it. Gilly got up again to tighten the drag right down and try to force the fish to come up. With so much line out, the line had enough stretch that just pulling on it wouldn't cause it to break. Gilly's boat was soon almost out of sight as they worked the fish.

A little while later I left the Near Side to head back for lunch. On the way I saw Gilly and Heck still out in the middle of the passage. The water there was much calmer and they drifted with the tide. They were both looking down at something on the floor of her boat. Curious, I took my guests over to have a look. I was sure we would see a tyee.

I pulled alongside. It was a big fish all right. Judging from the head, it must have been close to fifty pounds. But that's all I had to go by: the complete head of a very big salmon, plus a backbone and ribs and a huge tail. The backbone spanned the width of the boat, and the ribs stuck up into the air. It looked like all the flesh had been stripped away with a big melon baller. At the edges of flesh on the head and tail were round bite marks, evidence of a school of dogfish.

Heck sat staring in disbelief.

"Ain't that the goddamnedest thing you've ever seen, Dave? Look what they did to my beautiful fish. Gilly, she put me on a good one, but I just couldn't get it in the boat for her. She did everythin' she could. She was hitting the butt of the rod and we were pulling but them damn dogfish, there was just too many of them. We couldn't get it up, Dave, we just couldn't get it to come up."

His voice trailed off, choked with emotion. Tears welled up in his eyes as he looked down at the ruin that was his tyee.

Gilly wasn't mad about losing the fish, and she didn't blame the guest, as many guides might. Neither was she frozen and tight-lipped, not knowing what to do or say in the presence of such raw emotion. Instead, Gilly regarded him with a depth of compassion I had never seen on the face of a guide before.

It occurred to me that for Heck right now, Gilly was the best guide he could have. On top of all her experience with fishing and knowledge of these waters, she brought her own unique set of skills to the job. Of all the guides on the water around Stuart Island that day, she was the only one with any experience being someone's mother.

Gilly sat and waited as Heck wrestled with unfamiliar emotions, letting her boat drift in the current. There was something soothing about the rocking motion of the boat moving gently in the current. Gilly must have used this on her own child. She noticed as this understanding slowly took shape for me. She smiled and gave a nod, as if to say, yeah, it's okay, I've got this.

I let my boat slip quietly away and left them on their own.

thirty-six **KING HARVEST**

ON VOP'S LAST shopping trip, he had been a little distracted, so I took advantage of a day off to go to town myself. The day of Carl and Stephanie's big move was getting closer and I wanted to stop by and see how they were coming along. The house was up on land at this point and gumboots were no longer needed. The building sat on the rocky shore, a few feet above the water. I tied off next to it and climbed some temporary steps to the kitchen. I found Carl, dressed in black pajamas, having his morning coffee.

Now, people had the impression that Carl smoked a great deal of pot. It was certainly true; compared to the average person, he did, but it would be more correct to say he rolled a great deal of pot. Carl was always rolling something—pot, tobacco, breakfast burritos, whatever.

He rolled his own cigarettes out of a tin of Drum tobacco that was always on hand. In turn, he kept his day-to-day pot supply in the empty tobacco tins in a pantry cupboard. The tins had labels to show the date and time each of them was harvested. He liked to sample each in turn, to understand their different nuances. He had elevated the process of rolling into an elaborate ritual. He'd carefully measure out just the perfect amount of tobacco, or pot, and spread it evenly on the rolling paper. He might return some to the bag, then dip back in for just a tad more. He would pinch the paper together and roll it between his fingers and thumb. Perhaps not satisfied with the feel of it, he'd open it up and spread the contents out one more time. It was quite maddening to watch, even more so if you were waiting for him to roll you a fatty for the trip to town, as he was doing now.

Every once in a while, Carl would swipe at his now longish hair, which was now permanently plastered to the right side of his head. This whole rebuilding-the-float thing was causing some problems.

"It's going to be beautiful, man," he insisted when I finally asked. "People are going to talk about this for years. They won't believe it when it happens."

His hand reached up to his hair again. I could tell he wanted to talk about something else, anything else.

"Hey, do you have time to give me a quick hand? I've got some pot on the ridge above the house that really needs to be picked. I started it early in a greenhouse, and it's all ready to go now. It's going to be some of the best I've grown yet. Won't take more than half an hour or so."

I can recognize avoidance behaviour when I see it, especially from spending so much time with Vop. However, I was really curious to see his plants up close. And time wasn't an issue today.

Carl pulled on some sandals and the conical cedar hat Stephanie had woven for him. He tucked a couple of green garbage bags into his back pocket and we headed out. It didn't take long to reach the top of the ridge. In a small clearing left behind from a selective logging operation some years before,

Carl had set up some plants and surrounded them with a net fence to keep out the deer.

Carl opened up the net. He looked closely at the condition of the buds and pronounced them perfect. We started cutting the plants, laying them carefully on top of the bags to make up a couple of bundles. Before long, we had two equal sheaves.

That's when we heard the familiar sound of a helicopter approaching. There is no mistaking the "whop, whop, whop" of a Bell Huey, the type used by the RCMP. Carl reacted the moment he heard it.

"What are they doing? The cops aren't due to fly over here for another couple of days. Quick, man, grab a bundle and follow me. If the cops get overhead, they'll see the light green against the ground."

Carl scooped up one of the piles and headed to the trees. I grabbed the other and did my best to keep up with him. My heart was pounding, both from the danger of being busted and from the exertion of running over the broken ground. It seemed to take us forever to cross the clearing. Carl's hat blew off his head and hung by its string tie down his back. It bounced on his back as he ran.

When we were far enough under the trees, we threw ourselves under a large sword fern. We looked up as the helicopter passed overhead. The shadows of the fern cloaked our faces. The RCMP colours and markings on the side were clearly visible. We scarcely dared to breathe. Fortunately, they didn't notice us. The helicopter flew past, probably on its way back to the RCMP boat at Stuart Island.

thirty-seven   **A SLIGHT HITCH**

I WAS WORKING the day they moved Carl's house. People did talk about it, for years, even more than Carl could possibly have expected. Vop claims he even heard a folk song written about it. I talked to both Carl and Steph and heard their versions. It was pretty simple, really, to piece it all together.

That morning, the tug towed the barge with the crane on it into the bay. The tide was high, so the tug could position the crane barge right in front of the house, just like Carl's model. The skid logs under the house were then attached to heavy-duty straps, with one strap at each corner. A spreader to keep the straps from crushing the house was secured where the straps gathered above the roof. The massive hook of the crane caught up the four straps, and then the crane easily plucked the house off the rocks. Compared to what the crane usually moved, the house and all its contents weighed very little.

The full contents of the house remained steadfastly in place. Even Carl's prized Paris-made Selmer alto saxophone remained resolutely in its holder.

With the house suspended, the tug towed barge and crane gently away from the shore, again just the way Carl had envisioned with his Meccano model. The new state-of-the-art float was brought in and tied off to the shore, then the barge returned. It took some time to line up the exact spot where the house would be settled onto the float. The framework on which the house would sit was already in place and already decked in for added strength and rigidity.

The position of the crane and the float then took careful arranging. When the crane was ready to lower the house, everyone moved out of the way. People took up places to watch the event from the beach or from boats that kept their distance. Carl, Steph, and the movers also retreated to a safe place on the barge.

The crane operator had recently installed a twin disc transmission for his crane. It gave him the ability to power the loads down slowly, where previously the "down function" was strictly a brake shoe apparatus. Knowledge of these details, which went far beyond what he could have imagined with his Meccano model, only increased Carl's sense of confidence.

It was time to lower the house, and all eyes were transfixed by the scene. People held up cameras. Someone even ran a video camera to capture the moment.

The main structure of the house sat on two parallel logs. These logs rested on two more logs, one at either end, forming a box. Sometimes people drilled holes where the logs crossed, to bolt in long metal rods. These rods, or pins, stopped the logs from shifting while the house was being moved. A great deal of work was needed to drill these holes. If the house was only going to be dragged once onto a float, quite often this step was skipped. If you dragged the house carefully, just the weight of it was enough to keep the logs in place.

It was at this point in the proceedings that Carl's memory returned. He remembered the thing Steph asked him to check, and that he had put off looking into. Carl suddenly realized she was talking about the pins.

The house wasn't being dragged this time. It was forty feet in the air. Carl looked up at the house that hung in mid-air above him. It was so high above his head that he could now easily check what Steph had asked about. He didn't see any pins.

Carl had spent enough time with the models to know exactly what this meant. The house was sitting on top of the logs like a teacup on a saucer. The only thing that stopped the teacup from slipping off was the person holding the saucer. The crane operator had no idea that the straps on his hook were holding more of a teacup and saucer arrangement than a solid house and support.

Despite the new state-of-the-art clutch system, the operator still had to disengage it to reverse the cable system and let the load come down. It meant the house would drop a little before he could reengage the clutch. The house would drop and then he had to catch it, and catching it would cause a slight hitch.

Carl had to stop the crane right now. Maybe they could tie the logs together with some rope or cables, but the whole process had to stop. He lifted his arms and started waving at the crane operator.

The crane operator took it as a sign to start the drop.

If the house had been pinned to the skid logs, which is what Carl was supposed to look into, nothing would have happened. As the crane operator changed gears and caught the momentary free fall, the catch caused a slight movement of the house on top of the skid logs.

That slight movement was enough to unbalance the whole arrangement. One of the lifting straps crawled a little, and then the whole house flipped upside down. It landed with a huge splintering crash, dead centre on the float below.

Once the noise subsided, there was a stunned silence. No one could quite believe what had just taken place. Mouths gaped open. Everyone stopped taking pictures. The house was now a shattered pile of wood, glass, and personal belongings.

Into the silence began the sound of household objects dropping through the shattered roof and down the opening made for the house among the deck timbers, into the bay. One by one, something else would start rolling, find the hole and then land with a small plop in the water.

Everyone within hearing distance was affected by this sound, no one more so than the blind beagle standing at Stephanie's side. It lived in the world of sound. And it sounded like one of the dog's boxes of canned food had broken open and each can was now rolling one by one into the bay. With each plop, the beagle cocked her head to the side and let out a whimper of concern.

The only person who could believe what had just happened spoke up.

"Right," said Stephanie. "Any of you grinning idiots have anything to say for yourselves?"

All the men turned toward her. They knew exactly what she meant. Even men who had nothing to do with the move itself were caught with grins on their faces. They looked from one to another, then back to Stephanie. None of the grinning idiots had anything to say for themselves.

"Didn't think so," said Stephanie, with a slight touch of weariness.

Stephanie climbed down off the barge and onto the new float. She walked around the pile of debris, trying to get her bearings. Then she carefully picked her way into the remains of her house.

"Hey, you're not going in there, are you? There's nails and broken glass. Splinters," warned Carl.

"I totally appreciate your concern," Steph yelled back at him over her shoulder.

"What are you doing?"

Stephanie didn't answer immediately. She reached down into the mess and came up with a bag. She took another couple of very careful steps then reached down again. She pulled out an intact quart jar of smoked salmon and then another one. She dug around a little and retrieved two more unbroken jars of venison. She put everything into the bag.

Finally she said, "I'm thinking that by the time you guys get this mess on my new float cleaned up, you're all going to want something to eat."

She then turned and snagged a full bag of rice. Now carrying the beginnings of the evening meal, she made her way out of the mess that was once her home.

The crane operator and Carl had a quick conversation.

"Look, I know this is a disaster," said the crane operator. "But here is my idea. Jim and me will take the tug to Frederick Arm right now. There's a big log float there with a shed on it that the fish farm company owns. It just arrived and was going to be just stored. I can get it and lend it to you. I'll take personal responsibility for that, and we can be back here by tomorrow noon."

Meanwhile, the neighbours brought in their live-aboard workboat.

"Now you have water tanks, bunks, a heater, food in the cupboards, whatever you want, for as long as you need," they simply said.

The next day, boat after boat stopped by with food, tools, and labour. The salvage and cleanup proceeded quickly. Some things were lost, like the recently purchased propane fridge, crushed under a beam. Miraculously, the alto sax made it through relatively undamaged. The bell still has a bit of a kink in it to this day; straightening it further would've caused a crack.

That same day another friend arrived with an almost brand new aluminum landing craft, complete with a small loading crane. An employee of a boat-building company, he had heard about the disaster and headed over for the weekend with the best workboat they had. Now big chunks of the floor could be cut and lifted aside.

By noon the crane operator was back with another big float that held a closed-in shop building. By the end of the day, every salvageable item was stored under cover. In short order, a wood heater was working in the shop building. There was a new door on the room that was going to be the bedroom. All windows and drafts were chinked up and curtains hung. They had gravity water pressure, a gas generator, and a washing machine. The blind beagle had a brand new bed, a bone to chew on, and the reassurance of a never-ending supply of food.

thirty-eight # FOR SERVICES RENDERED

AT ABOUT THE same time that Stephanie was picking her way through the rubble that was her old home, a cruise ship approached Campbell River. It was Herbert Crane's recently refurbished Alaskan ferry, with 787 passengers on board. The car deck was filled with their cars, campers, and boats on trailers. One of the cars was a brand new Corvette Stingray; a number of people had brought special vintage vehicles for the drive along the beautiful coast.

This was day three of the maiden voyage. Everyone was settled in and enjoying the wonderful food and drink, the wonderful scenery. By all accounts, it was a great success. The people on board didn't have a care in the world.

As the ship entered Seymour Narrows, it came a little too close to Maude Island, perhaps pushed by the tide. The rocks below opened a thirty-foot gash in the hull. So much water poured in that the vessel was in danger of sinking. It turned around and crossed the channel to the Elk Falls Mill, just to the north of Campbell River, which had the only dock big enough to hold the sinking ferry.

The crew managed to get the ferry docked and the passengers safely off. But the vehicles could not all be removed and they were soon submerged in salt water. As the ferry sank and settled onto the bottom, it listed away from the dock. Under the strain, the dock, which had only just been replaced at great expense, ripped apart. The damage to the dock was so great that the mill had to shut down, affecting the entire economy of Campbell River.

A week later, a small group of Stuart Island guides, along with a couple from Campbell River, stood on the side of the road overlooking the mill. We silently took in the spectacle. The ferry still sat heeled over in the water, hundreds of feet of the brand new dock echoing its list. With so many layers of government agencies, insurance companies, and corporations involved, we observed the level of activity we had expected. Which is to say there was nothing going on. A couple of bored security guards wandered behind a makeshift fence, but apart from that, nothing.

"Wow, that's such a mess," someone finally said.

"Yeah, it's going to take weeks, maybe months, to clear all this up," said another.

"It's good no one was hurt. But I hear some really nice cars are a write-off."

"Everyone who worked at the mill has been laid off. Nobody knows when they'll get back to work. It's going to cause all kinds of problems."

Of course, Vop had to be the one to bring it up. "So, do you guys think Herbert was the one at th—"

"No," we all yelled as one voice.

"Hey, we all know where you're going with that." Trout-breath put an understanding arm over Vop's shoulder. "And none of us here would disagree with you. In fact, we're all trying hard not to think the same thing. But trust me, man, you can't say that out loud. Hell, you can't even think it. Besides," added Troutbreath, "I have it on pretty good authority that the pilot in charge has already submitted his bill for 'services rendered.'"

thirty-nine **TROUTBREATH AND THE DOLLY VARDEN**

"'GILLY THE GHILLIE.' Seriously? That's the best you can come up with?"

"Hey, come on, would you rather be known as 'That Cabin Girl'?" replied Troutbreath. "I mean, at least Gilly the Ghillie rhymes."

"That's important?"

"Absolutely."

Gilly, Nelson, and Troutbreath were on the gas dock sharing a joint of Carl's Time Warp from his latest crop. Gilly was teasing Troutbreath about nicknames.

"How did you ever come by the nickname Troutbreath? I mean, I don't even know what your real name is."

Gilly pointed to the oval patch on his overalls. Troutbreath was wearing a pair of the overalls he'd found, brand new, in a Campbell River thrift shop. Over the left breast was a large white patch with embroidered red lettering that said "TOM."

"I do know it's not 'Tom,' and as much as I hate to break it to you, you're not a 'Qualified Technician,' either."

Gilly was referring to the patch on another pair of overalls he had found that same day. Troutbreath was lucky enough to score four brand new pairs and he wore them on a rotating basis. He especially enjoyed it when unknowing customers referred to him as the "Qualified Technician."

"So how did you come to be known as Troutbreath?"

"I'm not sure I want to talk about it. It wasn't one of my finest moments up here."

"I'll let you call me Gilly the Ghillie, if that will make you happy."

"It's kind of a long story."

"What else are we going to do? The season is almost over and most of the yachts have pulled out. It's time for school to start up again, and I'm not ready for that. We need the distraction, eh? Come on. Troutbreath."

"Okay, okay. I'm surprised you don't know already. It was all Lucky Petersen. You see those Dolly Varden juveniles down there?" Troutbreath pointed to a small school of sea-going trout. They finned slowly, hanging in the current under the shade of the dock. "And you know how Mr. Carrington feels about the Stuart Island deer?"

"Are you kidding? He treats them like pets."

"Well, Lucky Petersen feels the same way about those trout. When I first got here, I made the mistake of catching one, then cooking and eating it. Lucky was quite horrified."

"Because you ate one? I mean, I've never caught a Dolly but they must taste good."

"Oh, no, never let him hear you say that. He has a whole twenty-minute explanation on why that's not a good idea."

"Seriously? I haven't heard him string more than three sentences together all summer."

"Just so you know the reason he is so protective, the poor little buggers used to have a bounty on them—two and a half cents apiece. They were fished and trapped relentlessly, supposedly to protect the young salmon. In Alaska, people collected the tails. Forty strung together on a wire was worth a dollar."

"Okay, now I'm starting to think you're just making this up."

"It's sad, but true," said Nelson. He was only too familiar with Lucky's thoughts on this matter.

"It is. You could use the strings to buy stuff in the stores, even for plane flights in and out of Ketchikan. The Dolly Varden finally had to be protected in Canada before they were fished to extinction. After I ate one, Lucky told me I had trout-breath now, and it kind of stuck."

"Lucky takes this stuff seriously, eh? You did warn me at the beginning of the summer. He's only recently stopped hiding in the bushes when he sees me on the path to the pub."

"That means you're well on your way to being fully accepted as a Stuart Island guide."

"Well, lucky me."

Nelson ignored the pun. He saw his opening and closed in on what he really wanted to talk about.

"So, you thinking of coming back here next summer?" Gilly had been a popular guide in the end and he liked to keep those around, male or female. The number of hours the yachting crowd had spent fishing was the highest it had ever been. It was mostly due to the increased interest of the wives, for which he gave Gilly full credit. Besides, he had been the one to give her a start.

"Oh, are you kidding? Of course I'm coming back next year. The money I made is really helpful, but you've got me hooked on the adrenaline. I've become an adrenaline junkie," she said, taking another toke off the joint. "I understand now. I know why all you guys put up with the downsides.

"Hey, I wanted to ask you. One of my girlfriends wants to try it next year. She's been fishing up here with her dad all her life. He's a pilot and he'd fly in to take her steel heading up on the Homathko. He flies people into Big Bay all the time. You might have flown with him. He has a gold front tooth? Anyway, she'd make a great guide. I mean, if I can do it, she sure can."

"Well, tell her to send me a letter. What's her name?"

"Her name is Heidi."

Troutbreath looked thoughtful for a few seconds, then a wonderful smile lit up his face.

"Heidi? Her name is Heidi?" asked Troutbreath. "That's perfect. I could have a Gilly the Ghillie and a Heidi the Geidi. Oh yeah, we'd better get her up to Stuart, no questions asked. She's going to fit right in."

forty

 **ERROR 18**

NELSON AND GILLY finished gassing up. Nelson ran back to the resort on Dent Island. Gilly wanted to settle up her tab before she went home to Read. After they had gone their separate ways, Troutbreath was left alone on the dock. Only two or three yachts remained at the resort. It was just before Labour Day, and the busiest time ended when the kids went back to school.

Troutbreath piled up some life jackets in the dock house. The afternoon sun was shining in through the side window, a raking light warming his makeshift bed. This summer hadn't left much time for lounging on a stack of life jackets. It really was his favourite place to be.

Troutbreath was just beginning to get comfortable when there was a shout from outside. He had to blink into the sun to see who it was. The two men on board a runabout stood waving in his direction. Troutbreath instantly recognized the two smiling faces. It was Lars and Gunnar.

Troutbreath quickly went out to greet them. As Lars tied up the boat, Gunnar explained that their yacht was down at the south end of the island, waiting for the tide to back off before coming into Big Bay. They had dropped the tender into the water to come up and visit rather than waiting.

Lars and Gunnar were from Sweden, where their family had developed a very successful packaging industry. Using the mathematics of the Egyptian pyramids, they had discovered a method for packaging food items that prevented spoilage for longer periods of time. They were well known in particular for the little packages of milk served in restaurants with coffee.

The study of ancient and rediscovered wisdom continued to interest them. They had the wherewithal to hire researchers to help them, and were very excited about some of their recent findings. While down in Fiji, they had explained to Troutbreath their latest project. In Sweden, as in other places in northern Europe, stones and stone circles could be found that held many mysteries. They learned how ancient texts made a number of references to the power these stones possessed. It led them to believe that some acted as portals. This was actually a fairly common belief in the Americas as well. If a person was attuned to its existence, a stone portal could transport them to another time.

On their first visit to Stuart Island, they found such stones. Perched on a ridge looking down at the tides, they saw petroglyphs etched in rock from thousands of years ago. The arrangement of the rock was very similar to what they had found in Sweden. The etchings were being deciphered and the preliminary explanation pointed to some kind of shift in reality.

This proved to be a very powerful spot. The Indigenous Peoples living here must have known it and memorialized the rocks with the petroglyphs. It was almost like a message put there for the future. Lars and Gunnar soon discovered they could travel through this portal. They had already done some careful experimenting in Sweden, but this site was much more powerful, and they came to an important conclusion.

The portal stones in Sweden were far from the ocean. Not only were these rocks in Canada closer, they suspected that the proximity of the rapids to the stones created an ionized atmosphere. The presence of such strong ionization increased the power and focus of the stones.

They had used some of the family fortune to create a device to help them open and hopefully control the portal. They hoped that with the device, they could tap into the power of the stones and, with more control, use it as a kind of time machine.

To begin with, they brought in only Swedish volunteers, who were sworn to secrecy. After getting to know Trout-breath during their time in Fiji, Lars and Gunnar felt they could trust him with their secret. They knew he was a man of discretion, someone who knew the importance of keeping this whole project quiet. Although he was initially quite skeptical of their claims, everything turned out to be exactly as they said. The stone portal controlled by their device really did create a time machine.

The portal didn't move you to a new location; it just shifted you in time. You stayed in one spot while time moved around you, like currents in the rapids. Troutbreath would always find himself in the same place on Stuart Island but shifted back to an earlier time. Lars and Gunnar were able to send Troutbreath to his time of choice, and so it was that he found himself returning, time and again, to a Stuart Island of the 1950s. He had wandered around in the house Dave and Vop lived in. It was clean and freshly painted; there were no cracks in the glass or things growing on the ceiling. The magazines lying around were all from about 1957 or 1958.

There were some minor problems with the time travel, of course. Troutbreath, as part of the deal, kept careful track of these for Lars and Gunnar. The first and most obvious problem, Troutbreath duly recorded as Error 1. A time traveller found himself back in time naked as the day he was born. Troutbreath found this very disappointing. He couldn't take back his favourite fishing rod and reel or even some fresh samples of Carl's latest harvest. Clothing would have been helpful also. The first few times he went back he'd had to skulk around in the bushes. So with the help of Lars and Gunnar, they tried to focus the effects. The portal was able to stop Troutbreath in a time from the past when no one was around. Through careful appropriation, Troutbreath was able to organize a small collection of necessities behind the house where Dave and Vop would live, and he could return to it each time.

The most exciting part for Troutbreath was seeing the cantilevered deck over the First Hole. It was newly built and he felt quite comfortable walking out on it. He could stand on it and look down at the whirlpools as they set up past the point. In the present day all that was left of it were some rotting timbers and the chains and heavy iron staples that anchored it to the rocks.

Outboard motors in this time were rare, and people rowed out to fish in the back eddy. They would arrive at the First Hole at slack tide and stay there for the entire tide. They had to wait until it was safe to row back again. Putting yourself at the mercy of the tide in a rowboat was incredibly dangerous. The rowers couldn't chase the fish out into the tide. They stayed in the back eddy and played the salmon from there. They used heavy-duty rods, like pool cues that could hold fishing line. The line was sixty-pound test so the fish couldn't break it. Basically, all they were doing was using the gear like a winch to drag the fish up to the boat. If they lost one, it didn't matter. There were so many fish, they just dropped the line again and caught another one. Once the deck was installed people could use it just as easily as a rowboat.

Most days Troutbreath wouldn't even want to harass the fish. He liked to arrive on days when the sun shone, warming the boards of the deck. He could sit and watch the tide go past and enjoy the peace and quiet. No sound of float planes landing or taking off, no buzz of guide boats or chainsaws, just the rustle of the tide and the occasional whickering cry of a real eagle. Time would drift by for hours.

Troutbreath found that even if he spent an entire day in the past, when he returned to the present only a few minutes had passed. He couldn't believe his good fortune. Finally, he could reclaim the peace of his early days as a dock boy. He could spend the day messing about near the ocean, maybe doing a little fishing, or just taking a nap in the sun.

There were other more unsettling problems with time travel that Troutbreath preferred not to think about. Error 18 was the one that scared him the most. Sometimes Troutbreath would end up in a different time, farther back than expected. Vop and Dave's house wouldn't be there, nor would any of the other houses. The trees were all first growth. He had travelled back before the island was logged. Lars and Gunnar were most concerned about this discrepancy. They had run into problems with some of their Swedish volunteers. Troutbreath was always happy to feel the rocks collect him and bring him back to his own time.

"You guys ever go into the future?" Troutbreath asked Lars and Gunnar once. They both shook their heads and exchanged glances.

"We tried that with a couple of the Swedish volunteers using the stones here, but we had to stop doing it almost immediately. The results were not what we expected. There were too many variables. The travellers often didn't return to the point of origin properly. It was like there had been some kind of seismic change in the future. And the volunteers—the volunteers themselves came back changed somehow."

Lars and Gunnar said they had been trying to locate the last of those volunteers. It was the reason they were back in the area this late in the season. Happily, they had finally tracked him down. After completing a great deal of paperwork and forms, they had finally been able to retrieve him from the psychiatric wing of the Campbell River Hospital. They'd put him on a plane back to Sweden that morning. Troutbreath vaguely remembered a story from the beginning of the summer about some strange guy Vop found living under a log.

They offered to send Troutbreath back one last time before the summer ended. It was a pleasant walk out to the location. The instruments took a moment to set up and Troutbreath found himself back in time once more. Unfortunately, Error 18 occurred and took him away from his usual place of comfort.

Troutbreath appeared, as usual, on top of the small rise above the water where the stones were. But he was surrounded by the telltale first-growth forest. Below him a totally unexpected scene unfolding before him. A beautiful wooden clinker-built boat floated near the shore, its thick white paint so clean and fresh that it shone and sparkled in the afternoon sun. He had seen pictures of such boats in history books, and even the remains of one or two in maritime museums, but this one was almost brand new. It was a beautiful example. In fact, the paint was so fresh and thickly applied, Troutbreath wondered if someone hadn't ordered a little too much of it and had to find a way to use it all.

He had access to quite a bit about the history of the area in the books Lars and Gunnar kept in their library. One of them detailed the logbooks that Captain George Vancouver kept on his 1792 voyage. From the clues of the boat, and a few other things, Troutbreath decided he was looking at a ship's boat, or pinnace, belonging to a much larger sailing vessel on that voyage of discovery.

The beautiful boat gleamed in the summer sun, its new canvas sails lowered. A full complement of sailors manned the rowing stations, oars held in the ready position. One man, red faced, slightly out of breath, and wet up to his waistband, was standing just on shore holding the bow rope to keep the boat from floating away.

Behind a tree directly in front of Troutbreath, someone with their back to him was taking a leak. He was a youngish fellow, probably in his early thirties. If a blue macaw had landed in front of Troutbreath at that very moment, it couldn't have looked more out of place than this man. He wore a blue jacket with gold trim and polished brass buttons, standard English naval issue of the 1790s. He had an elaborate tri-cornered hat and wig assemblage, as precariously balanced on his head as Carl's float house had balanced on the skid logs. On his feet he wore black patent leather shoes, each with not one but two buckles.

The guy holding the rope cleared his throat to get the attention of the officer. He nodded in Troutbreath's direction.

The zipper would not appear on men's trousers for another one hundred and thirty years or so. Before the officer could turn around to see what his sailor was trying to signal, there was a great deal of folding, tying up, and buttoning to be accomplished. When he finally did spin about, his hat came into contact with a low branch. The whole wig-hat arrangement on his head was knocked ever so slightly askew.

"You there," he said, pointing to Troutbreath. "What do you mean, skulking about behind me like that? I am Acting Lieutenant James Johnstone of His Majesty's Ship *Chatham*, here on important business for the king. State your purpose!"

The man stood there with his hands on his hips. He was used to issuing orders to people. Troutbreath understood this guy at once. He had just spent the summer dealing with people just like him.

From his study of history, Troutbreath knew these guys were here without even the benefit of a gas station road map. They were sailing in what for them were uncharted waters. They had somehow managed to make it through the rapids in their delicate wooden boat. Troutbreath also knew the only reason Mr. Johnstone was able to navigate this far and not have his beautiful sailboat reduced to just so much well-painted kindling was the local knowledge and assistance provided by the Indigenous Peoples he had encountered along the way. His boat had been towed and pulled along from the shore by the men whose ancestors had been living here for thousands of years, but that didn't stop him from blithely claiming for his king everything he saw.

While all this realization was taking shape in his head, Troutbreath struggled with a couple of the effects of time shifting. First of all was Error 11. It was usually just an inconvenience: each time shift left his face feeling numb for a few minutes. He had trouble moving his mouth and tongue properly, as if he had just been to the dentist. It passed quickly, and normally didn't bother him. But he had never materialized directly in front of people before, and these people were expecting him to answer questions. He stood there with his mouth frozen open, trying to look friendly.

Troutbreath realized he had a much more subtle problem than just being unable to use his mouth properly. He couldn't just chat up an English naval officer from the age of sail as though he was another customer at the gas dock. Standing there gaping and stark naked in front of the man, Troutbreath knew he had to come up with something. He could never begin to explain to this person what was actually going on. To open his mouth and speak clearly in English would not do. The man before him would immediately assume he was some kind of a deserter. That would mean, at best, a long uncomfortable trip in the hold of the HMS *Chatham* to an equally uncomfortable bed at Bedlam Hospital, if they didn't flog and hang him instead.

Thinking quickly, Troutbreath hoped that with his long hair and lack of clothes, he might be mistaken as another helpful member of the shore patrol. But he had to proceed carefully.

The officer in front of him was getting impatient.

"Squires, McCrippen. That man!"

Two dour-looking gentlemen sitting amidships stood up. Troutbreath recognized their red tunic and black top hat as the standard uniform of the Royal Marines. They were equipped not with oars but the short-barrelled naval version of the Brown Bess musket. They dutifully leveled their guns at Troutbreath.

Troutbreath was only too aware of the danger here. The Brown Bess was a .75-calibre smoothbore flintlock that fired a slug that weighed a little more than an ounce. While the gun wasn't accurate at longer distances, at such close range and in the hands of two well-trained marines, it would be hard to miss. The prospect concentrated Troutbreath's mind wonderfully.

"Ah, ah." Troutbreath struggled to make his mouth work. It did sound like he had just come from the dentist. To disguise his true origins, he tried to think of the most Indigenous-sounding thing he could think of.

"Ah, ah..."

"Well, come on, speak up man!"

One final desperate effort and Troutbreath managed to blurt out, "Ah, Saskatoon Saskatchewan."

"What's that?" There was a short pause. "Oh yes, of course," said Acting Lieutenant James Johnstone of His Majesty's Royal Navy. "Nothing but more of that local gibberish. Well, never mind, we'll have you speaking the proper King's English soon enough. Squires, McCrippen, stand down. Moffat!"

He turned away for a moment, ordering poor Moffat back into the freezing water. "Get this man a blanket, some good English broadcloth, that he might cover his nakedness."

Fortunately, Troutbreath felt the familiar draw of the stones pulling him back into the present. When Mr. Johnstone turned back, Troutbreath had vanished.

Later that afternoon, when Lars and Gunnar's family yacht made it into the bay, Troutbreath had a chance to dip into their library again. He pulled up their copy of Vancouver's log and found the entries relating to Mr. Johnstone and his time in this part of the world. The little hairs on the back of his neck stood to attention as he read.

Mr. Johnstone had succeeded in finding his way into the
arm leading to the westward through the narrows, where
they were assisted by the friendly natives, about a league to
the south of the passage by which he had before entered it;
making the intermediate land, lying before the entrance into
Bute's channel, nearly a round island three or four leagues
in circuit, which obtained the name of STUART'S ISLAND.
This channel was not less intricate than the other, neither of
which he considered a safe navigation for shipping, owing to
their being so narrow, to the irregular direction and rapid-
ity of the tides, and to the great depth of water; which, even
close to the shore, was no where less than sixty fathoms.

[As for] the character and general deportment of the few
inhabitants we occasionally saw, they were uniformly civil
and friendly, without manifesting the least sign of fear or
suspicion at our approach; nor did their appearance indicate
their having been much inured to hostilities. Several of their
stoutest men had been seen perfectly naked, and contrary to
what might have been expected of rude nations habituated
to warfare their skins were mostly unblemished by scars,
excepting such as the small pox seemed to have occasioned;
a disease which there is great reason to believe is very fatal
amongst them.

forty-one **THE RAIN BARREL**

WHILE TROUTBREATH WAS unhinged from his place in time, Vop was just unhinged. Today was the day he and Carol took possession of the house on Cortes, as its legal owners. Guiding was mostly done now. Vop wanted to winterize his things in the cabin on Stuart Island, and then head down to Cortes. Carol was already there, airing the house and getting it ready for the party that night. Vop was more than looking forward to it.

Getting the Stuart Island cabin organized wasn't easy. Vop was still a little dazed by all that was happening. He found himself wandering from one room to the other and then trying to remember why he was there. Only through strength of habit and routine was he able to accomplish anything at all, and it took him twice as long as he expected. When he finally headed out, there wasn't much daylight left.

His guide boat couldn't go fast enough. The tip of Cortes almost seemed to be running away from him. Vop headed to the small deep cove north of the house, where a permanent float was moored. When he finally arrived, the small dock was already crowded and he had to tie up to the outermost boat.

The sounds of a party in the distance floated up the steep finger of land separating the tie-up dock from the house. Vop started down the trail that passed behind the storage buildings and the woodshed. At the bottom, the trail stopped and turned, and the route continued along a walkway from the woodshed to the house, past the rain barrel that collected water from the woodshed roof.

It had been a long day and Vop was a little too excited. As he came down the hill his feet got away from him. For a guy who complains that the universe is out to get him, he lost focus, and the universe saw its opportunity.

He tried hard to stay on the path, even hopping on one foot in a vain attempt to keep his balance. He almost made it to the step over to the walkway. It was not enough. He tripped and plunged head first into the barrel, which was full to the brim after the wet summer.

As things quieted down, Vop immediately realized he was in a bit of a predicament. Not only was he head first in a barrel filled with water, but his arms were also pinned to his sides. He couldn't use his hands to push himself out and he couldn't breathe. In fact, he was in danger of drowning. Only his best black gumboots remained above the surface of the water, soles facing up.

Vop knew no one inside the house had heard him fall into the water. He couldn't expect any help from there. It was up to him to solve this. It's not that Vop was afraid of dying. He was afraid of dying a stupid death. He had never wanted to be one of those people whose last words were "oh shit!" It was more about his friends. He didn't want one of them to find him head first in a water barrel with his best black gumboots pointed to the sky.

Vop started to struggle. He found he could rock the barrel by shifting his weight from side to side. He could feel the barrel wanting to tip over. He rocked back and forth tipping the barrel more and more each time. Finally he felt the barrel fall and all the water rushed out. Vop took a huge gulp of air. He was on his back staring up at the inside of the barrel. It took him a moment to recover.

That's when the barrel started to roll down the hill toward the ocean and a drop of some twenty-five or thirty feet from the bank to the rocks below. The barrel bounced along on the rough ground, gaining speed as it went, Vop spinning and bouncing right along with it. Right at the edge, the barrel hit a small arbutus tree and stopped.

Vop was now dazed from a slight concussion. The barrel had broken up when it hit the tree and Vop extricated himself from the wreckage. He grabbed the salal bushes he had just rolled through to pull himself back up to the walkway. He had to sit on the boards and wait for the world to stop spinning. It was a couple of minutes before he could find his way to the front door of the house.

The party was already in full swing. As he tottered up the walk, the door was flung open and a couple of people embraced him.

"Hey, everyone," someone yelled back into the house. "Vop's here."

Carol appeared beside him.

"Oh good, you made it." She wrapped her arms around him, and then let go immediately. "Vop! You're soaking wet. What have you been doing?"

Before Vop had the chance to explain, Carol continued, "Tell you what—never mind, I don't want to know. It's better if I don't. Look, come on in and let's get you some dry clothes. Hey, you guys, Vop's here."

Vop allowed himself to be dragged in front of the fire, wrapped in a blanket, and settled into a warm, comfy chair.

Someone put a beer in his hand and someone else handed him a joint. Vop was home. For the time being at least, he was safe from a universe that conspired to kill him.

 *forty-two* # THE TROPHY WALL

THE NEXT MORNING, while most of the people at Vop and Carol's place were still sleeping, Mr. Breland took the elevator to the top floor of his office building in Vancouver. The elevator opened right into his expansive penthouse office, which had a panoramic view of Stanley Park, downtown Vancouver, and the mountains of the North Shore. It was intended to impress, a place that showed off his power and accomplishments. It was a place to seal the deal.

Today, Saturday, would normally be a day off. However, Mr. Breland had something important he wanted to do. He had brought a few tools and some cleaning products from home to help accomplish the task. He stopped in front of a showcase of framed objects on a prominent wall opposite the expansive picture window. It featured diplomas and certificates, testimonials, and thank-you letters, all made out to Mr. Douglas Breland. There were photos of him with presidents of the United States, Canadian prime ministers, and influential cabinet members; with athletes, hockey players, and coaches; with well-known Canadian and American celebrities and movie stars—all people who had helped him raise money for charities. The pictures were autographed and dedicated to

Mr. Douglas Breland. It was a display not unlike many others in offices all across the country.

Mr. Breland removed some of the objects, putting them out of the way on his desk. He rearranged a few others, cleaning and dusting them as he did so. He repositioned hangers for several of the photos. Some pieces were carefully moved to a display shelf below. He stood back and considered the space he had opened up more or less in the middle of the wall. Satisfied, he pulled out a small item from the pocket of his coat. It was wrapped in tissue paper.

Most executives had treasures much like he the ones had on the wall, autographed pictures of a president or a celebrity, degrees or certificates from universities. But what Mr. Breland held in his hand was something special. None of the other walls he visited at his friends' or competitors' offices had anything like it.

He carefully unwrapped it and fixed a hanging clip to the back. He hung it in the special place he had just arranged for it. Mr. Breland stepped back to admire his handiwork. He knew the kind of attention this little object would generate, and he didn't know if he was ready to live up to it.

Amid the expensively framed photographs, with their gilding and double mats, now hung a cheap brass plaque, tacked at each corner to a piece of driftwood, just a sun-bleached piece of wood anyone could find on any beach on the West Coast. The brass plaque was inscribed with these words:

WINNER
Stuart Island Community
Salmon Derby
Doug Breland
46.5 pound Spring Salmon
1984

EPILOGUE

BEHIND DENT ISLAND Lodge, where tourists and visitors seldom venture, a small clearing has been scraped out from the surrounding bush. Curiously, the remains of a forty-foot outrigger canoe have been laid to rest there. The bushes are already beginning to reclaim the clearing. A small plaque attached to the top of a four-by-four explains why it is there.

In the summer of 1972 four Americans, three men and a woman, brought the canoe up to Stuart Island. One of the men was a writer for *Life* magazine. Their intention was to run the Arran Rapids at full flood on the biggest tide of the year and then write about the experience for the magazine. Any of the locals who heard of their intention tried to talk them out of it. The outrigger canoe was ungainly in the rapids, no doubt better suited to sailing across the Pacific. Most of the locals who saw it declared it a death trap.

Despite all the warnings from the people who worked on that water every day, the four people persisted. With a twenty-horse outboard for power, they headed straight down the middle of the channel at full flood. They didn't last long in the big whirlpools. Almost immediately, the tide caught the canoe and broke off the outrigger, and the whole rig flipped over. Somehow, the woman managed to hang on to the overturned hull and was rescued at the other end of the rapids but the three men were never seen again.

The remains of the canoe are starting to decay. Wood rots pretty quickly on this coast. You can still make out the colours the canoe was painted. Once bright and optimistic, they are now peeling and faded. A small monument to hubris, it too will eventually surrender to the elements. The plaque might last a little longer. Perhaps some visitor will find it, push aside the overgrowth, and wonder about the story and whom this might represent. It is more likely that it will just quietly disappear until just such a plaque is needed again for just such a monument.

ACKNOWLEDGEMENTS

ANOTHER BOOK FOR Kim. Her love, support, and encouragement makes it all possible.

A special thanks to Howie for letting me use the house story, and helping with some of the details, even if it was a little too soon.

Thanks to Dave W., who actually was my roommate at the Big Bay House and may or may not have been the inspiration for some of the stories.

Thanks to Lenore, who helped make me a better writer, and thank you to the people at Heritage House who make it all happen.

More from David Giblin

The Codfish Dream
Chronicles of a West Coast Fishing Guide

ISBN 978-1-77203-242-0 (pbk)
ISBN 978-1-77203-243-7 (ebook)

AFTER SPENDING FIFTEEN years as a fishing guide on the BC coast, David Giblin decided that the offbeat people and places he'd encountered during that colourful period in his life had to be preserved. Like any good fishing story, wherein the fish seem to grow faster after they are dead, the forty-seven interconnected narratives in what eventually became The Codfish Dream took on a life of their own. The result is a series of hilarious, strange, keenly observed, true (or mostly true) stories of Giblin's experiences. These whimisical tales are held together by a thread of international intrigue that affects everyone in the small community of Stuart Island over one eventful summer, when FBI agents visit the island to investigate insider trading. The Codfish Dream is an unforgettable book imbued with an undeniable sense of place and time.

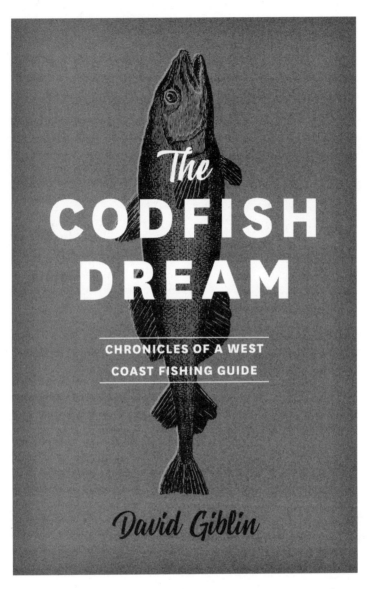

The CODFISH DREAM

CHRONICLES OF A WEST COAST FISHING GUIDE

David Giblin

Visit heritagehouse.ca to see this and many other similar titles.

ABOUT THE AUTHOR

DAVID GIBLIN was born in Norwich, Norfolk, England. His father, a merchant seaman, ran away to sea at the age of sixteen and worked on the North Sea on a Norfolk sail-powered fishing boat, and later on freighters that visited Vancouver and Port Alberni. In 1957, when David was six weeks shy of his sixth birthday, his family moved to Canada. He grew up in Horseshoe Bay, on Vancouver's North Shore, and began messing around in small boats early on. In the '70s, while living on Cortes Island, he heard about Stuart Island from a neighbour who worked as a cook at Big Bay Marina. He did his rookie year there before getting his own boat and going independent. He worked as a guide for fifteen years, the last five as head guide at Stuart Island Resort. This book, like The Codfish Dream before it, grew out of the stories the guides would tell. David studied art at the University of British Columbia; Kootenay School of the Arts (now Selkirk College); Capilano College (now University), with Allen Wood; and Victoria College of Art, under Jim Gordaneer and Bill Porteus. He lives in Cobble Hill, BC.